THE ROMANTIC EAST

THE

ROMANTIC EAST

BURMA, ASSAM, & KASHMIR

WALTER DEL MAR

GYAN

Published by

Gyan Publishing House
5, Ansari Road
Daryaganj, New Delhi-110002
Phone: 011-47034999, 9811692060
E-mail: books@gyanbooks.com

Distribution Network
gyanbooks.com
India, USA, Canada, UK, Australia, France

ISBN: 978-81-212-8386-1 (PB)
First Published, 1906

2nd Impression 2023

Printed at: Gyan Press, Delhi.

THE ROMANTIC EAST
Author: WALTER DEL MAR

THE ROMANTIC EAST

Photographed by Taber, London.

WALTER DEL MAR.

THE ROMANTIC EAST

BURMA, ASSAM, & KASHMIR

BY

WALTER DEL MAR

AUTHOR OF
'AROUND THE WORLD THROUGH JAPAN' AND 'INDIA OF TO-DAY'

CONTAINING SIXTY-FOUR FULL-PAGE ILLUSTRATIONS
FROM PHOTOGRAPHS

LONDON
ADAM AND CHARLES BLACK
1906

PREFACE

The Romantic East is a narrative of a tour in Burma, Assam, and Kashmir, and it completes the series begun in *Around the World through Japan* and continued in *India of To-day.*

The romantic side of Burma is to be found in its people, who are of all Oriental races the least spoiled by contact with the West. The romance of Kashmir lies in the country itself, while the romance of Assam is a purely commercial one, connected with the tea industry.

The Romantic East offers some guidance as to what may be seen during a short tour; and it will serve a useful purpose if it induces those who intend to travel at some future time to mature their plans in the present, for now is the time to visit Burma and Kashmir—before the character of the Burmese people is changed by the steady influx of alien immigrants, and before the amenities of the Kashmir Valley are endangered by the new railway.

The majority of the illustrations are from my own cameras, but several are selected from the large collection of Burmese photographs taken by Mr. W. W. Schumacher in 1905. The design on the cover represents a corner of the Eindawya Pagoda, Mandalay.

CONTENTS

LIST OF ILLUSTRATIONS

FACING PAGE

THE ROMANTIC EAST

CHAPTER I

GOLDEN BURMA

The ideal East—Burmese characteristics—The Yellow Peril—Annexation—Religion—Marriage and divorce—Burmese women—Costumes—A few figures.

In Ptolemy's map of the world, dating from the second century of our era, Burma is marked Chryse Cherson, "The Golden Peninsula." Then, as now, its streams were worked for gold ; but so little is now won from the alluvial deposits that its ancient name would no longer be appropriate if it were not for its pagodas. These lift their gilded spires all over the country, and justify not only its Greek but its Indian title of Souverna Bhumi, "The Golden Land."

It is to-day, of all countries open to easy travelling, the nearest approach to the ideal East, the least spoilt, in spite of its oil-mills, rice-mills, and timber-yards, by contact with the West, and the most pleasing in regard to the character of its people.

These conditions, however, are doomed to pass away. The Burmese, originally Indo-Chinese, are being hard pressed by their ancestral races. By the northern frontier and from over the seas the enterprising Chinamen pour into the country in a steady stream, absorbing the retail trade of the rural districts, and competing successfully in the towns; while the famished hordes of Tamils come over in their thousands to cultivate the paddy-fields of the delta and press the idle Burman from the land.

Up to the present no great harm has been done, for in spite of the undesirable aliens the Burmese continue to increase. The coolies employed in the towns are doing work which the Burmese never attempted to do, and the Chinese are rather forcing the Burmese women out of business than competing with the men. The Burman is by heredity and choice a cultivator of the soil, and as a field labourer is unexcelled. But now he is being

Photographed by the Author.

"ALIEN IMMIGRANTS."

attacked in his last stronghold by the Tamil, and the struggle may prove disastrous to the Burman, either on the material side, or by causing a change in his most pleasing characteristics.

By nature the Burman is an indolent, lazy fellow, who is quite willing to let his wife do all the work without any interference on his part as long as she provides him with plenty of food to eat and tobacco to smoke. But the idleness of the Burman, fostered by a superstitious belief in lucky and unlucky days, is not the shiftless indifference of the ne'er-do-weel or the sullen apathy of the weak and hopeless. It is rather the careless optimism of the philosopher combined with the sportsman's contempt for productive labour inherited from a long line of freedom-loving ancestors. For the Burmese were a conquering race, their empire had been successfully defended by the sword from the assaults of the surrounding hostile races and tribes; and when the British took Burma they found a free race who had not, as in India, been previously subdued by foreign invaders.

Watch the Burman play at his favourite games, or put him in charge of a boat on a river in flood, and you will find that he has a fund of energy to expend on those things in which he takes an interest. Moreover, he is a cheerful, merry fellow; and, when not roused to sudden jealousy, a very pleasant companion. But John Chinaman is taking to wife the pick of the Burmese girls, and he has his privilege of selection, because he gives them a better home, less work, and finer clothes and jewels; and, as long as his sons' pigtails are left to his care, is quite content to conform to the observances of the Buddhist religion, and let his wife bring up the daughters as she likes. The mixed race springing up from these inter-marriages is a very good one indeed, inheriting the cheerful temper and quick wit of the mother together with the father's capacity for work. To the Chinaman Burma is China inasmuch as he is content to live, die, and be buried there, and you may meet Chinamen whose fathers and even grandfathers have been born in Burma. John is not far wrong either, for Burma was, at any rate nominally, tributary to China as recently as 1881, or up to within five years of the time when England took the third bite and gobbled up what had been left of the Burmese cherry from the two previous bites taken in 1826 and 1852.

By the treaty of February 24, 1826, the coasts of Tenasserim bordering on Siam, and of Arakan, the narrow strip between the mountains and the Bay of Bengal, were ceded with the outlying bits of Assam to the Honourable East India Company by His Majesty the King of Ava. By proclamation of December 20, 1852, Lower Burma was annexed, and the Irawadi valley up to Prome, as well as the valley of the Sittang up to a point about thirty-five miles north of Toungoo, came under British rule. On January 1, 1886, Upper Burma was annexed, and the whole of Burma became a province of British India.

Upper Burma was the real home of the Burmese race, Lower Burma being occupied by the Talaing or Mun race; but the Burmese have settled in large numbers in the delta, and it is becoming more and more difficult to distinguish the various races which inhabit the country.

Practically all of the Burmese are Buddhists; but the missionaries have had considerable success with some of the minor races, and it is said that a round hundred thousand of the Karens are Christians. In theory, Burmese Buddhism is the purest form of the religion, unchanged since it was brought to Burma by Asoka's missionaries, and it is possible that some of the more learned monks follow "the way" indicated by Gawdama; but, as a rule, the Buddhism of the Burman is so lost in a flood of superstition that it is rarely found on the surface. The Burmese have, however, learnt from their religion the virtues of tolerance, charitableness, kind-heartedness, and hospitality to a degree beyond most other races. Even the casual visitor to their country is impressed with their romantic character and envies their happy disposition.

As in other Buddhist countries marriage in Burma is a purely secular affair. The parties agree to become man and wife and that is quite sufficient. If there is any ceremony at all, the most important observance is the eating out of the same dish, just as the Japanese drink out of the same saké cup. The wife retains her maiden name and her separate property. Divorce is equally simple and free. In the villages an application to the elders by either party procures a divorce attested in writing: the

Photographed by Watts & Skeen.

A PROFESSIONAL BEAUTY SMOKING A "TORCH."

party claiming the divorce leaving the common home. Each retains the property he or she had before the marriage and half of what has been accumulated during the time they have been husband and wife. In some cases where the husband has paid "marriage-money" to get his bride the wife must repay this if she secures a divorce. In any event, the wife takes the female children and the husband the male children.

There seems to be no law against a plurality of wives nor any stigma attached to having two or three wives under the same roof. In these customs the Burmans and Japanese agree, and in Burma as in Japan the family life of the peasants is open to the observation of any traveller.

Burmese girls have little of the educational advantages of the boys, but their free life gives them an early worldly knowledge, and the Burmese women have many attractions. They are affectionate and passionate, cheerful and bright, clever in their own affairs and in business, sharp in making a bargain, excellent housekeepers, and generally faithful wives. They are seldom public prostitutes, but a girl may be bought from her parents. The negotiations are usually conducted with the mother, who is keener at driving a good bargain ; and when the contract is made the girl is kept as a concubine, and does not lose caste by assenting to such an arrangement. During her concubinage she is treated as, and usually called, a " wife," and she frequently brings her mother and the children of previous "marriages" to live at the house of her new " husband."

The Burman drapes himself in a paso, or putsoe, which is a piece of cloth about fourteen feet long and forty inches wide, and twists a gaily-coloured handkerchief around his head.

The costume of a Burmese woman ordinarily consists of two pieces ; the engyi and lungyi, or tamein. The former is a loose double-breasted jacket with mandarin sleeves and falls over the lungyi, which, whenever the wearer can afford it, is of thin silk and is simply a square of about five feet with the ends usually sewn together so that it is put on like a petticoat and folded in over the right hip. Women usually go barefooted, but sometimes wear clogs resembling the Japanese *geta*, or ornamental slippers with a pointed toe-cap which holds all but the little toe. Decorated with a

Photographed by W. W. Schumacher.

TAKEN BY AN AMATEUR.

certain amount of jewellery, with a scarf (*ta-bet*) around her neck, a wreath of flowers in her well-brushed hair, and a bunch of "Christmas orchids" falling over her right ear, the Burmese girl makes rather an effective picture; but you must be careful not to annoy her by aiming your camera at her, as she has an idea that with it you may be able to see through her clothes, a liberty which as a modest and moral girl she can't allow. The older women generally wear one or two switches or tails of false hair, and rub the face and neck over with white powder when making their toilet.

The Burmese year 1267 began on the 15th of April 1905, and the fact that their era is so far behind ours may account for their not being quite up to date in some other matters. For example, it took us the best part of two days to do eighty-three miles by rail; it took until Wednesday afternoon for a letter posted the previous Friday in Rangoon city to be delivered round the corner; and it took over a quarter of an hour and a personal application at the office to get a clean towel at the leading hotel in Burma. But there are compensations, as we discovered the morning we left Mandalay for Gokteik. The train leaves Mandalay at six in the morning to make the connection at Myohaung, and we had engaged a ticca-gharry to call for us at the Club in time to catch this train. But it seems that the gates of Fort Dufferin are not opened until six o'clock, and, owing to this, our gharry arrived too late for the train. However, we drove to the station, caught a train at 6.30 A.M. to Myohaung, and found the train for Gokteik still waiting at the junction, where it continued to wait for another quarter of an hour.

Including the Shan States, which are "more or less dependant," Burma has an area of 236,738 square miles, or over four times that of England and Wales, and its population in 1901 was estimated at over 10,490,000, while the cities of Rangoon, Mandalay, and Moulmein had respectively 234,801, 182,498, and 55,785 inhabitants. Rice is the principal food of the people as well as the principal article of export; and of the total cultivated area, which exceeds 11,000,000 acres, three out of every four acres are planted with rice. When we left Rangoon at the end of December, 1904, we were told that nearly 2,300,000 tons of cargo-rice would be available for export during 1905, an amount that would be reduced by fifteen per cent in converting it into cleaned rice. Not only is the delta extremely well adapted to rice-growing but the heavy rainfall, averaging from a hundred to two hundred inches at various places near the coast, is another favourable factor.

In Burma we found that we were "thakins" instead of "sahibs," and that we were honoured with a *sheko* in place of a *salaam*.

CHAPTER II

THE FIRST VIEW

Madras to Rangoon—The Rangoon river—Plague protection—Pagodas and dagobas—The fraternity of the Yellow Robe—Monks and monasteries.

UP to the time we visited Burma there had been no plague in that country and, as a protection against it, passengers leaving Indian ports for Rangoon had to be examined by the Health Officer at the time of embarkation, and their servants had to present themselves, four or five hours before the steamer sailed, for personal examination and fumigation of their clothes and luggage; an indignity which our "bearer" strongly resented.

We sailed from Madras for Rangoon, in a "British India" steamer, going out to the ship in a jolly-boat, and did the voyage of nine hundred miles in a few minutes over three days. Our

Photographed by the Author.

"WHITE WINGS."

vessel, of about 4000 tons gross and under 2000 tons net, is licensed to carry, if used for natives only, over 3500 passengers, on and 'tween decks, in fair weather, and nearly 2000 in foul weather. On this voyage we carried about 1800 Tamils for the rice-fields of the Irawadi delta, and in addition there were untold numbers of ants, cockroaches, and rats aboard. The voyage was without accident save that a Jesuit priest left open the bathroom tap, which flooded all the cabins on one side of the ship and damaged a lot of clothing and luggage.

At eight o'clock in the morning of the third day we sighted the lightship on the Krishna Shoal, at three o'clock in the afternoon we slowed up at the pilot brig and took the pilot aboard, an hour later we had the obelisk on Elephant Point abeam and at six o'clock in the evening had landed on the pier at Rangoon.

Entering the Rangoon river we overtook a full-rigged ship carrying every stitch of canvas, a glorious sight seldom seen in these days. Farther up we saw the rice-boats and house-boats with the high sterns peculiar to Burmese rivers but not unlike the Chinese boats seen on the Canton river. The sampans in the Rangoon river also remind one of China, but the boatmen row Malay fashion standing and pushing their crossed oars.

It is eleven miles from the pilot brig, or about seven miles from the first buoy which marks the channel of the Rangoon river, to Elephant Point at its entrance, and Rangoon is twenty-six miles farther up the river, or twenty-two miles as the crow flies. The obelisk on Elephant Point is 130 feet high, and the Eastern Grove lighthouse on Grove Point opposite is 93 feet high. On the way up the Hmawwun (Mowoon) Chaung enters from the east, and a little higher up Bassein Creek joins from the west. Liffey Island is passed, and just before the Pegu river comes in from the east the Syriam Pagoda is seen on the same side. Syriam, the old town where the Portuguese, Dutch, and English had in succession factories or trading-posts, lies some miles away up the Pegu river.

The first distant view of Shwe Dagon pagoda, rising above Rangoon and dimly seen through its smoke and haze, is one of the most impressive sights that can well be imagined. It awakens the feelings of awe and veneration inspired by the view

Photographed by Watts & Skeen

BURMESE BOATS.

of St. Paul's from the lower Thames, or the white dome of the Capitol at Washington seen miles away over the tops of the trees. You may, in very clear weather, first get sight of the pagoda from the bridge of a steamer while still out at sea; but it is more likely to come into view, after entering the river, about three miles above Elephant Point, when it is still over twenty miles away by boat.

The Shwe Dagon is the largest and most famous of all the Burmese pagodas, and the pagodas are the most characteristic feature of Burmese scenery. Every prominent cape on the coast of Lower Burma, and almost every hill in the Irawadi delta is crowned with one, and every village has one or more, while in Upper Burma they are found in great numbers in Mandalay, the modern capital, and in Ava and Amarapura, two of the previous seats of Government. They are to be seen scattered up the river valleys to the very borders of China, and although they differ from the so-called pagoda of the latter country, they form an architectural link between them and the dagobas of India and Ceylon.

The nine-storied pagodas on the Canton river

are in reality towers of victory, and each story has its projecting roof or cornice, closely resembling the projections on the Burmese pagoda spires. The Burmese name for pagoda is zedi, and paya means a shrine or its image.

Both the pagoda and the dagoba are lineal descendants of the tope at Sanchi, and to the great Asoka, the builder of the Indian monument, Burma and Ceylon owe their architecture and their religion. The Buddhists say that Asoka sent the missionaries Sono and Uttaro to convert Burma, and that Buddhism became the Burmese state religion in the second century of our era; but Western historians think that Buddhism was introduced into Burma three centuries later from Ceylon. In both countries practically the whole of the indigenous population remains Buddhist to this day, those who profess other religions being immigrants or their progeny.

The Burmese pagodas are similar in general form to the Thuparama Dagoba, at Anuradhapura, and others of the same type in Ceylon; and, like the dagobas, are gigantic reliquaries built over some sacred object. They are not only identical in the main outlines of construction and in the use of solid brickwork throughout, but even the name pagoda is supposed to be only a corruption of dagoba, which in turn is supposed to be derived from the Sanskrit words dhatu, relic, and garbha, womb. In both cases a raised platform, almost invariably square in plan, is built, although in some cases, as in that of the pagoda on the Botataung jetty at Rangoon, the top of the platform is on the, present, level of the ground. From the centre of the platform the pagoda proper springs, conical or pyramidal in general form, but most frequently with a square sub-base changing to a diminishing or terraced octagonal base, and then into a circular form tapering to a point surmounted by an umbrella-shaped metal top called a ti which sometimes has the shape of a miniature seven or nine-storied pagoda.

The dagoba usually has a circular base on a square sub-base, but more nearly approaches a hemispheric form; and is also surmounted with a ti differing, however, in minor details from the pagoda ti. The processionals or space left on the platform between its outer edge and the base of the dagoba proper is sometimes ornamented with statues, as at the Ruanweli Dagoba, Anuradhapura, and enclosed with an ornamental rail, while the pagoda platforms are more frequently embellished with smaller pagodas, shrines, or bells suspended on wooden frames.

The relic, if a very holy one, would probably be encased in gold, then enclosed in a silver box, which would in turn be placed in a copper receptacle, and this would be embedded in the centre of the erection, sometimes at the level of the platform and sometimes higher up. After the solid brickwork had been finished, the fabric would be covered with stucco or some sort of plaster, which would be whitewashed and perhaps covered with gold-leaf. In some cases a small pagoda containing a precious relic is completely encased in a larger pagoda built over it at a later period, and this process may continue until the original platform becomes the base of the enlarged pagoda.

There are some further peculiarities of the Burmese pagodas to be noticed. The base is sometimes completely encircled with minor shrines, as is that of the Sule pagoda, Rangoon, or kept entirely free, as is that of the Eindawya pagoda, Mandalay. Sometimes the embellishments of the platform follow some definite plan and are part of the original design, but more often these additions are made in an irregular and haphazard manner. Moreover, while the building of a pagoda or a shrine is a sure way of "getting merit," the same result is not attained by an equal expenditure in repairing an old one, so that you may see, on the same platform, shrines in all states of repair, from the freshly painted and gilded shrine with the carvings sharp and intact to the tumbledown shed with dismantled top, decayed boards, and defaced carvings. So with the pagodas themselves: some are overgrown with trees, and some show their brick bones through their torn stucco skin, some are black with age, while others are newly white-washed or raise aloft glittering spires of gold.

Shwe is the Burmese word for golden, but is also in general use to indicate anything superlative, and whether a pagoda is entirely covered with gold-leaf, or partly gilded, or has only a gilt ti, its name is pretty sure to begin with shwe.

After the pagodas the greatest architectural

interest lies in the pongyi-kyoungs, the monasteries or residences of the pongyis or mendicant monks, who shave their heads, and, clothed in yellow garments, beg their daily food. Their vows are taken for a short period only, but may from time to time be renewed indefinitely, or may be terminated at the end of any specified period. The monasteries or pongyi-kyoungs are not only the dwelling-places of the monks, but the schoolrooms of the country, so that every Burmese lad in former days followed the life of a monk for some years, and many Burmans return to it in after life. Even to-day primary education is almost entirely in the hands of the monks. A layman may become a monk at any time, and a monk may become a layman at the termination of the period for which he has taken the vows. In this manner the life of the monks is known to the people from the inside, and there is no mystery about it.

Every Burmese boy entered a monastery as a probationer or sheng when he was eight or nine years old, and assumed the yellow robe of a novitiate at about the age of twelve. The four grades are called sheng (or shinlaung), yahan, goyin, and

Photographed by W. W. Schumacher.

BURMESE MONKS.

pongyi (or monk). The rank of pongyi is only properly applied to those who have had ten years' service in the monastery. Nuns are not numerous, and therefore few Burmese girls got any regular schooling. The monks are not priests, but simply men who are following the path of virtue leading ultimately to Nirvana (Nehban). They take upon themselves no priestly functions, although they teach the spiritual law, expound the scriptures, and exhort others to keep from sin and follow the holy way.

CHAPTER III

RANGOON

The Shwe Dagon pagoda—Gawdama the Buddha—Tagon-daings—The great bell of Rangoon—The story of the tiger.

As the Shwe Dagon was the first Burmese pagoda we had seen in the distance, so it was the first we visited after landing at Rangoon. We drove out by the Pagoda Road, which is a continuation of China Street, passing the cathedral, the level racecourse, and the cantonment gardens, and dismounted at the foot of the long flights of stone and brick stairs leading from the south side to the top. On the first terrace going up, two monster griffins guard the entrance, which is through a new seven-roofed pavilion decorated with teak carvings and gorgeous in fresh paint and gilding. Then the steps lead up through passages to the levelled top of Theinguttara Hill, which forms the great platform and measures 900 feet by 685 feet. From the centre of the platform rises the pagoda on an octagonal base measuring 1355 feet around.

The height of the pagoda is given by different authorities at various figures from 320 to 370 feet, and the height of the ti above the sea at from 448 to 574 feet. The City Survey and the *Gazetteer* agree that the latter elevation is 513 feet and the Survey gives the details as follows: Crown of road at south steps 103·98 feet above mean tide, platform 83·77 feet above road, rim of the talapoin or umbrella 295·55 feet above platform, and tip of ti 30·38 feet higher. The metal ti, which therefore rises about 326 feet above the platform, and is forty-seven feet high and weighs 2800 pounds, was presented in 1871 by Mindon Min, King of Independent Burma. It is heavily gilt and studded with jewels, and it is believed to have cost £62,000.

The Buddhist legends claim that Dagon, the name of the city until changed to Rangun by Alompra, King of Ava, was founded in the sixth century B.C., and that the pagoda was built to contain relics of Gawdama and three previous

Buddhas. The sacred relics include the staff of Kakusanda, the water-filter of Konagamana, a portion of Kasyapa's robe, and eight hairs from the head of the Buddha, given with his own hand to the Burmese envoys.

The base of the pagoda, from which the gold-leaf put on in 1871 has mostly disappeared, is entirely surrounded by temples and shrines, most of them containing brass or marble images of the Buddha in the act of renouncing the world. The Shwe Dagon has been regilt several times during the last century, and the gold required to do the work well is alone worth nearly £10,000, to say nothing of the labour involved.

The Burmese name for the Buddha is Gawdama (or Godama) from the Sanskrit *Gautama* or Pali *Gotama* ; and from the other Indian name of Sakya Muni the Japanese get their name of Shaka and the Chinese get Sa-ka. The latter also call the Buddha Fo, Foe, Fo-hi in their different dialects, and the Japanese commonly use the word Butsu. In Burma the standing Gawdama is called Mat-tat-kodaw ; the seated one, with the right hand over the knee and the left held palm upward in the lap,

Photographed by W. W. Schumacher.

CARVED BASE OF TAGON-DAING, SHWE DAGON, RANGOON.

Tin-myin-kwe; and the reclining, dying Buddha, Shin-bin-tha-yaung.

Many of the Gawdamas in the Shwe Dagon shrines have gold-embroidered robes thrown over their shoulders and covering them to their feet. The shrines themselves are covered with stucco, decorated with coloured glass, and have plate glass fronts, or are built entirely of teak. If of the latter, the wood may be in its natural colour, or varnished, or stained black, or gilded. At the side of these shrines are stone or stucco elephants, lions, and other beasts; and dotted about are tagon-daigns, or flag-staffs, carrying the peculiar cylindrical or flat streamers made of netting held out by splints of bamboo.

On the opposite side of the processional path surrounding the pagoda, or rather on the outer margin of the platform, to the right of the south entrance is a beautifully carved pavilion with thirteen pillars holding aloft double spires of seven stories. On the east side of the platform is a white temple, having in one bay a reclining figure of Yathodaya, the wife of Prince Theiddatha, the Buddha, reposing on a handsomely decorated charpai, over which are suspended three modern white silk parasols trimmed with lace; and some of the best teak carvings are to be found on this side of the platform. On the north side is a carved and gilt pavilion with handsome pillars. In one of the corners near the Shan pagoda is the shrine of the great bell, or Maha Ganda, "the great sweet voice," 14 feet high, 15 inches thick, and 7 feet 7½ inches in diameter at the mouth, which was presented by Mentara Gyi;—and thereby hangs a tale. In 1853, after the second war with Burma, the British conquerors attempted to transport to Calcutta as a trophy this bell, which weighs over 42 tons and is said to be the fourth largest in the world, but the boat overturned and the bell fell into the Rangoon river, and there remained despite all efforts to raise it. So the Burmans asked if they might keep the bell if they could get it up, and the official reply was, "If (with heavy emphasis on the if) you can raise it, you can have it." Now the Burmans had no heavy tackle, but they had a small idea whose application solved the problem. They made a heavy disc of solid teak, the exact size of the bell's greatest diameter at the lip, and

Photographed by W. W. Schumacher.

SHRINE ON SHWE DAGON PLATFORM.

fastened it firmly to the other end, or ear, of the bell, and in that manner made a wheel of it. They were then able by passing ropes around the centre to roll the bell out of the river and replace it on the temple platform. This is the accepted story, but the fact is that Maha Ganda was never moved at all. It was a smaller bell hanging near the north-west corner of the platform which was seized by the prize-agents during the war of 1826 and abandoned in the river. Sir James Edward Alexander, then a subaltern, in his *Travels*, published in 1827, relates that the natives raised the bell "by attaching two cables to it, which at low water were made fast to a brig moored over it; when the tide rose so did the bell, and was hauled ashore."

There is another story of more recent date in relation to a tiger, which in some unexplained manner found its way into Rangoon, and sought refuge on one of the terraces of the base of the Shwe Dagon pagoda. Down rushed the monks and temple attendants in a panic to the fort below the pagoda and implored the soldiers to come up and kill the ferocious beast and so save them from a terrible death. After much difficulty and some danger the tiger was traced to its hiding place, and in order to get at him a soldier had to climb to the roof of one of the smaller shrines from which he killed the animal. Next day there was a great commotion. The very pongyis who had begged the soldiers to kill the tiger denounced them as wicked slayers of the temple's *nat* or good spirit, and not only hung the skin over the spot where it was shot, but ultimately placed on the pagoda platform a plaster image of the tiger to be worshipped by the faithful and shown to the curious.

On the west side is a tazoung or memorial chapel, erected by Ko Oung Gyee (Gyi) in 1900 at a cost of Rs. 120,000 (say £8000), which will serve to show the quality of recent work as compared with the older examples here. On this side is the great recumbent Buddha, whose temple was being regilt at the time we visited it, and near the north-west corner is a big seated Buddha. To the right of the shrine at the top of the entrance steps is a finely carved tusk in a glass case.

Even more interesting than the carvings on the shrines or the images within is the crowd of well-

Photographed by W. W. Schumacher.

WOMEN'S TRESSES OFFERED AT SHWE DAGON SHRINE.

behaved worshippers who throng the platform. The Burmese women stroll about smoking cheroots or "torches," the latter nine inches long and an inch in diameter, containing a mixture of tobacco and leaves rolled in a teak-leaf wrapper or in a piece of the inner bark of the betel-tree.

The Burmans lie on their back in the shade of the pagoda and smoke all day. Even children only four or five years old smoke, and you may see a Burmese woman offer a puff from her "torch" to her friends or acquaintances. At one shrine you may see a party of worshippers from the north-west frontier of India, at another some pilgrims from Siam or Ceylon; and you will be almost certain to see a resident Chinaman with his Burmese wife and children, the boys wearing pigtails and the girls dressed in Burmese fashion. On the platform are fortune-tellers, and on the way down are the shops for flowers, sweets, candles, tobacco, and the triangular gongs with a wonderful tone which you may buy for a rupee, as well as quaint pith dolls, who stand on their elephantine legs, which are on sale from an anna up. Then there is the drive through Dalhousie Park, where you may see the syces holding sunshades fashioned like the ancient chhatra or royal umbrella over the mem-sahibs; and there is the view, so well known from sketches and pictures, of Shwe Dagon over the Great Royal Lake (Kandawgyi).

Photographed by Watts & Skeen.

THE SULE NAT, SULE PAGODA, RANGOON.

CHAPTER IV

RANGOON—(*continued*)

The Sule pagoda—Nats—The Central Jail—Teak and elephants —Silver-ware—Rangoon hotels.

THERE is another famous pagoda in Rangoon, the Sule, at the junction of Dalhousie Street and Sule Pagoda Street. Under this pagoda a Talaing prince is said to have been buried alive by Alompra. The well-kept pagoda platform contains many brass Gawdamas, and at the south-east corner is a shed under which may be seen the image of the Sule Nat, the guardian angel of the Shwe Dagon. The Burmese firmly believe in nats and their great powers for good or evil. There are nats with the attributes of good fairies or angels to be prayed to, and nats like evil genii or demons to be propitiated, but the existence of both kinds is very real to the Burmese, and the belief in them underlies their Buddhism and is not affected by the adverse teachings of Gawdama.

One of the sights of Rangoon is the Central Jail, capable of accommodating three thousand prisoners and holding nearly two thousand at the time of our visit. There were prisoners at work as carpenters, blacksmiths, printers, bookbinders, mat-makers, cabinet-makers, wood-carvers, and rope-makers; and at the jail showroom, opposite the entrance, can be bought the results of their labour. The carved teak furniture is worth buying, but you must estimate an amount equal to the original cost for shipping expenses to your home in London. If it goes farther, or to a country where there is an import duty on such goods, more must be allowed for expenses. The gallows in the jail-yard are built to remain in position permanently, and we saw some Burmans in the cells under sentence of death. The prisoners all have fetters rivetted to their ankles, and if refractory are punished by being put to work on a windlass working a grinding-mill, or by flogging. We heard the groans of one poor

Photographed by the Author.

RANGOON JAIL, OUTSIDE THE ENTRANCE.

wretch being flogged while we were making some purchases of "long-sleeve" chairs and carved teak purchases in the showroom. The flogging is done with a rattan half an inch thick and about a yard long.

Rangoon is on the left bank of the Hlaing or Rangoon river, just above the point where it receives the Pegu river and Pazundaung creek. On the banks of the latter most of the rice-mills are situated, while the oil business is concentrated on the Pegu. The unhusked rice, or paddy, is converted into cargo rice by grinding off the outer husk, or into milled, or white rice by denuding it of the inner pellicle as well. Higher up the Rangoon river, half-way to the suburb of Kemmendine, are some of the big timber-yards. Having procured a card to the manager of one of these yards, we went out early one morning to see the elephants at work. They are unable to endure the heat during the middle of the day, even in winter, so that in the cold season they are only worked from daylight to nine o'clock and from three o'clock to dusk, while in summer their working hours are shorter.

The mahout sits not on the elephant's neck, but on a sort of cross-frame of wood placed on a padded cloth well in the centre of the elephant's back, and uses a long light goad (*guzbuz*); but well-trained animals learn to understand and obey, without being ridden, half-a-dozen words of command. We saw three at work, one old warrior whose brittle, chipped ears betrayed an age of eighty years or more, a young one, and one in his prime, about forty years old. They dragged the logs out of the river and up to the saw-mill with chains; lifted them off the ground with their trunks and tusks; pushed them with their fore-feet, hind-feet, or trunk as directed, and finally stacked the squared timbers exactly as required. On the way back there are the fine carvings of the Chinese joss-house in the Strand Road to be seen, and at the other end of the Strand Road, which continues as Monkey Point Road, is the Botataung Jetty, where there is a gold pagoda whose platform contains monuments erected over the graves of British soldiers and sailors who fell in the second Burmese War more than fifty years ago.

We spent most of one day in a ticca-gharry

Photographed by W. W. Schumacher.

TIMBER-YARD ELEPHANTS, RANGOON.

driving about Rangoon and its suburbs, but failed to find anything further of great interest. The dilapidated pongyi-kyoungs at Kemmendine, one of whose shrines was in use as a stable, are hardly worth the journey. There is nothing extraordinary about Government House; or the private bungalows in Park Road and other fashionable avenues; or the clubs, unless it be the sheds used as beggars' clubs; or the bazaars, except that it is curious to see how the business there is monopolised by the sharp and clever Burmese women.

A visit to the silversmiths in Godwin Road was interesting as showing how stationary the art has remained. Almost the only articles on sale are silver bowls cast in the rough and finished on the outside by hand chasing. It is a fact that we saw no *repoussé* work being done, as all the artisans were at work chasing, but we were unable to verify the statement that none of the bowls are worked from the inside. However, the bowls are nearly all made with the same conventional designs, and their value largely depends upon the work and art displayed in the chasing. We were shown one or two specimens of pierced work in silver, but could not find any niello work. In the latter the chasing is filled in with black niello, an alloy composed of lead, silver, copper, and sulphur.

All, from the poorest workmen to Maung Yin Maung "Master Silversmith," ask double the weight of the article in rupees, a price which only the latter should get for his very finest work. Even supposing the silver in the bowl to be of standard fineness, it is only worth twelve annas per tola instead of sixteen; so that buying silver articles, even at their simple weight in rupees, means giving a profit of thirty-three per cent on the cost of the silver. As this method of selling worked silver by weight is in use all over India from Burma to Kashmir, it may be well to explain the calculation in detail. The rupee is of British standard silver and weighs exactly one tola. The tola weighs 180 grains or $\frac{3}{8}$ of an ounce troy. Therefore when bar silver of standard fineness is worth $26\frac{2}{3}$ pence per ounce the silver in the rupee is worth $\frac{3}{8}$ of $26\frac{2}{3}$ or exactly 10 pence. For the silver in the rupee to be worth a shilling, bar silver must sell at 32 pence, to be worth the present par of 16 pence (or annas), bar silver would

Photographed by W. W. Schumacher.

STREET SCENE, RANGOON.

have to rise to $42\frac{2}{3}$ pence per ounce; and to be worth the old par of 2 shillings, to 64 pence per ounce.

Rangoon hotels afford interesting studies for the naturalist. In the course of one evening you may discover in your bedroom striped squirrels, chirping lizards, and muskrats, to say nothing of fleas, mosquitoes, ants, and cockroaches. From your windows you can see black crows, vultures, and, in the distance, cranes as well as other wading birds.

NOTE TO CHAPTER IV

The Ava Kings of the Alompra Dynasty

1753. Alompra.
1760. Naung-daw-gyi, Tsit-kaing-meng or Upa-yaza, eldest son of Alompra.
1763. Maung Lauk, or Sinbyushin, second son of Alompra.
1776. Maung Ye Hla, or Singu Min, eldest son Maung Lauk.
1781. Maung Maung, or Paongoza, reigned a few days, only son Naung-daw-gyi.
1781. Bo-daw-paya, Mentara-gyi, or Maung Waing, fifth son Alompra.
1819. Ba-gyi-daw, grandson Bo-daw-paya, went insane 1830, deposed 1837, died 1845.
1837. Tharawadi Min, brother Ba-gyi-daw, went insane 1845.
1846. Pagan Min, son Tharawadi.
1853. Mindon Min, brother Pagan Min.
1878. Thebaw Min, son Mindon Min.

CHAPTER V

RANGOON TO BHAMO

Pegu—The Shwe-hmaw-daw—The great Buddha—Karen women—Toungoo — Amarapura and Ava — Sagaing — Katha—Shwegu.

TOURING in the interior of Burma is difficult unless you stick to the routes followed by the Irawadi Flotilla steamers or to the railways. The latter are metre gauge, with a total length of 1353 miles in May 1903, and the principal projected extensions, for which the Government is to provide £1,500,000, are from Pegu to Martaban, opposite Moulmein, 122 miles, and from Henzada 68 miles to Kyangin, on the Irawadi. Burmese standard time employed on the railway is six hours and thirty minutes ahead of Greenwich, or one hour ahead of Indian standard time.

On the way to Mandalay by the railway you can, between the trains, visit Pegu, the ancient

Photographed by Watts & Skeen.

SHWE-HMAW-DAW PAGODA, PEGU.

capital of the Talaing kingdom of Henthawadi. Pegu was once a port, and is still connected with the Sittang river by the Pegu-Sittang Canal which joins the river at Myit-kyo. The city was destroyed by Alompra nearly a hundred and fifty years ago, but of its former greatness two wonderful monuments remain, the colossal Buddha to the west of the railway and the Shwe-hmaw-daw pagoda.

Long after the dome of the Rangoon secretariat has sunk below the horizon, you can see from the train the Shwe Dagon, which is visible as far away as Dabein, over twenty-two miles from Rangoon by the railway, while at Tawa, nine miles from Pegu, the Shwe-hmaw-daw can be seen from the left hand side of the train. From Pegu station you are driven about a mile by way of Slaughter House Road, the Bridge, Canal Road, and Thanatpin Road, passing a great number of wheelwrights, whose houses have an open lower story, used as a store-room or stable, with the living apartments above. You pass the Leik-pya-gan tank on the right of the road on the way to the pagoda's south entrance, which latter was newly painted and lighted in 1901. The square platform is only 10 feet above the fields, and measures 1390 feet each way. The second platform is 20 feet higher, has a perimeter of 2736 feet, and can be entered by stairs in the centre of each face. The octagonal base of the pagoda has sides measuring 162 feet each, and the ti rises to a height of 324 feet from the second platform.

The Shwe-hmaw-daw is a graceful bell-shaped pagoda, surmounted by a pyramidal metal ti hung all around with tinkling bells, and it is covered with gold-leaf in various states of preservation, the most recent renewal being on the highest octagonal part, where bamboo screens had been erected to protect the gilders who were at work during our visit. The smooth circular part above was also bright and comparatively fresh. The carvings on the cornices of the seven-story wooden tower on the platform are excellent; but on the whole there is not much to be seen at Shwe-hmaw-daw beyond the pagoda itself, which seems out of place in a town whose population is now only about 14,000, and the pagoda would be deserted but for the pilgrims who come from a distance to worship at its shrines.

Photographed by W. W. Schumacher.

THE GREAT RECLINING BUDDHA, PEGU.

On the way back we turned to the right at the canal to visit a pagoda with a large and well-executed brass Buddha, and then continued across the railway to the Shwe-nadaw pagoda, and the Shwe-guzale pagoda with its sixty-four Gawdamas, and afterwards by a shocking bad road to the Shwe-tachaung or great Buddha, which is also known as the Shin-bin-tha-hlayaung. This is a reclining figure over 180 feet long, and 50 feet high at the shoulder. At the head, which bears a peculiar head-dress or tiara called magiak, is a large box. The figure and its pedestal are of brick covered with plaster. It had been entirely lost sight of and overgrown with jungle until it was discovered in looking for ballast for the railway. Since then the plaster has been renewed and freshly painted over, the box at the head, and the finger-nails of the Buddha have been gilded, and the head-dress decorated with glass jewels. Near the head are erected two tagon-daing of bamboo, sustaining long cylindrical streamers of split bamboo covered with paper, which reach to the ground when there is no wind. The bare glimpses of this colossus, which could formerly be obtained from the railway carriage just before reaching and just after passing Pegu station, are being shut off by a building, with steel lattice pillars, under construction to protect it from the elements. Its direction from Pegu station is between a conical pagoda near at hand, and the square Mahazedi farther off to the west. The Kyaikpun pagoda with the great seated figures, 90 feet high, of the Four Buddhas, lies to the south, and beyond it the Shwe-ku-gyi pagoda.

In Pegu we saw many Burmans wearing only a loin cloth, and had our first opportunity of studying at close quarters the designs with which their bodies were tattooed, some few from neck to instep, but most of them from the waist to the calf of the leg. There is a curious story, told by Sangermano but denied by Symes, in relation to the origin of the universal Burmese custom of tattooing the body, which ascribes this custom to the wise king who commanded the young men to be tattooed, and the young women to wear their lungyis so as to expose one thigh, as they are still sometimes worn in Mandalay. The object was to encourage marriages and increase the declining birth-rate. The Karen women who live in the Pegu district, and come

Photographed by W. W. Schumacher.

THE PAGODA OF THE FOUR BUDDHAS.

(Note the man standing by the right-hand Buddha)

originally from the Salwin valley, are said to be the least moral of the native races, and most of the prostitutes in Burma are said to be recruited from them.

Going north from Pegu a stream is crossed before reaching Shwehle; and between Pyuntaza and Nyaunglebin there is a gigantic seated Buddha, under a rough bamboo and matting shed, near the railway. The Kaboung river is crossed two miles before reaching Toungoo. This town, which is on the right bank of the Sittang river, was at one time the capital of an independent kingdom and remained the terminus of the railway until after Upper Burma was annexed. East of Toungoo the Myalat range of South Shan hills come into view and continue until Kume Road station, some of the peaks being nearly 5000 feet high. Pyinmana is the centre of one of the teak districts, and its big pagoda shows up well in the morning sun, while at the next station hills are to be seen to the west. At Nyaungyan, near the top of the watershed between the Sittang and Irawadi rivers, 624 feet above the sea, there is a very effective group of pagodas to be seen from the station.

There is a halt at Yamethin, and it is in the plains to the east of this town that the Sittang and Tsamon rivers rise, the former flowing southward between the Pegu and Paung-Laung hills, 350 miles to the Gulf of Martaban, and the latter flowing northward 100 miles into the Myit-nge, just above its junction with the Irawadi. The Sittang river is famous for its "macareo" or bore, which is similar to the eagre of the Trent and the Severn. This phenomenon is caused by the action of the tides which rush up the river in the form of a wave, and in the case of the Sittang this wave at the river's mouth is ordinarily about three feet high and travels against the stream at a pace estimated at twelve miles an hour. This bore must have become greatly modified, unless the early writers on Burma, who state it to have been fifteen to twenty feet high, were given to some exaggeration.

Thazi, 306 miles from Rangoon, is the junction for the branch line to Myingyan which passes through Meiktila, where there is a famous lake. At Myittha we saw a number of Shan women wearing wide trousers and great umbrella-shaped straw hats, and a few miles beyond we crossed the

Zawgyi river with its stone weir, from which the town of Kyaukse takes its name. Above the town is a hill covered with scores of white pagodas and crowned with the gilded Shwethayaung. At the station the pedlars were selling "sugar corn" (maize) and the native policemen were armed with swords. The Myit-nge is crossed before reaching the town of the same name with its cluster of pagodas. There are a vast number of pagodas to the east of the line near Tagundaing, the station before Myohaung junction where the three lines—to Mandalay, to Lashio, and to Amarapura Shore for Alon and Myitkyina—centre. We followed the latter branch, changing at Amarapura for the ferry across the Irawadi to Sagaing.

The river at Ava, four miles lower down where the Myit-nge enters and about 700 miles from the sea, is nearly five-eighths of a mile wide. Ava was formerly the capital of Burma, during the reign of Bo-daw-paya, and it was from this ancient city that the first Marquis of Dufferin and Ava took his title in 1888 after the annexation of Upper Burma, which took place during the time he was Viceroy of India. After Ava was deserted Amarapura became the capital until 1860, when the seat of Government was removed to Mandalay.

The view of Sagaing from Amarapura is extremely picturesque, and seen in the evening sun, its gleaming pagodas gave back the light from every eminence, including the hillocks close to the river, to the distant mountain tops, and ranging from Nga-dat-gyi near by on the west side to the great round dome of the Kaunghmudaw in the north. We clambered up the ghat at Sagaing, followed to the station by a crowd of girls and women carrying our luggage, and we amused ourselves by purchasing samples of the fruit on sale there. Pineapples, bananas, custard-apples, pomegranates, and kamrakh, or carambolas, were to be had, the latter a bitter fruit having a four-pointed star on the top and better suited for cooking than eating raw. Between Sagaing—which was the capital of Burma in the fourteenth century—and more recently during the reigns of Naung-daw-gyi and some of his successors—and Ywataung, the modern railway town three miles away, there is a pagoda with a tree growing from the top. There is also a large brick dome-shaped pagoda, surmounted with a ti, called the Kyewa ("breast") pagoda to be seen north-west of Ywataung station.

The railway runs north up the Mu valley, and to the east can be seen the hills which separate this valley from the valley of the Irawadi. We passed Shwebo, the seat of Alompra's government and his burial place, during the night, arriving at Naba junction early in the morning, and changed there for Katha, where we caught one of the river steamers which wait till noon if the train is late and run daily to Bhamo. We had planned to go up to the terminus of the railway at Myitkyina, 724 miles by rail from Rangoon and 138 miles from Bhamo by river, and come down by river to Mandalay, but we found that no steamers ran above Bhamo, and that travelling by native boats was uncomfortable and uncertain.

The systems of transliteration from Burmese to English generally place the letter y after a consonant, to show that the latter is soft but it nevertheless comes as a shock to hear Myitkyina pronounced so as to rhyme with Kitchener, and gyi "great," pronounced the same as jee. For reasons known only to the learned, Amarapura has the tonic accent on the first syllable, while Pegu, Katha, and Moulmein have it on the last syllable.

The time-table of the Irawadi Flotilla is subject to daily change during the winter months, owing to the prevalence of fogs, especially in the mornings, so that you cannot be at all sure where you will cast anchor or tie up at night, or when you will start the next day. The steamers only run, as a rule, while there is daylight, and it takes on an average about fourteen hours' steaming up stream from Katha to Bhamo, and about nine hours down. Leaving Katha about 10 A.M. we passed the Government of Burma's elephant kheddahs (kheda) on the west bank and reached Moda, thirty miles above Katha, in three hours. At 5.30 P.M. we stopped, half-way between Katha and Bhamo, at Shwegu, a pretty village with picturesque pagodas, flagstaff, and kyoungs perched up high above the river on a bluff from which long flights of wooden stairs, one with sixty-five steps, come down to the water's edge, and we lay up at Sinkan, below the second defile, for the night. The next morning we put off at half-past five, but a heavy fog came down at six o'clock, and we had to cast anchor for an hour and

Photographed by W. W. Schumacher.

SHWEGU ON THE IRAWADI.

a half, and even then could only move slowly ahead, while the Chittagonian "leadsman" took soundings with his bamboo pole, and sung his droning refrain of *Ek bahm kam ek palm* "one fathom less one palm." However, we arrived at Bhamo fairly early and had nearly the whole day to see the town.

CHAPTER VI

BHAMO AND THE IRAWADI

The road to China—The races of Upper Burma—Chins—Shans—Kachins—Palaungs—The river—The defiles—The road to the Ruby Mines—The Mingon bell and pagoda—Petroleum.

BHAMO, the ancient capital of the Shan state of Manmaw stretches along the left, or east, bank of the Irawadi for four miles. It contains a mixed population of Kachins, Burmans, Shans, and Chinese, numbering over 10,000 in 1901, and its population and trade are rapidly increasing owing to its favourable position as the nearest mart on the Irawadi to the Chinese frontier.

Three miles above Bhamo the Taping river enters the Irawadi, and the road into China goes up the Taping valley about 125 miles to Momien (Teng-yueh-ting), where the road from Myitkyina joins. From Bhamo, which the Chinese call Tsingai, by way of Momien and Ta Li Fu (the Carajan of

Marco Polo) to Yun-nan Fu is 450 miles, and there is a good road for 80 miles ; while from Yun-nan Fu are mule tracks connecting with the roads entering the Yang-tsze valley. From Bhamo to the Yang-tsze is about 800 miles by road, and on to Pekin 950 miles more. It takes nearly four weeks to go from Bhamo to Ta Li Fu, and from Ta Li Fu to Yun-nan Fu twelve days.

Owing to low water the river channel was full of sand-banks, and the steamer had to tie up below the ghat, near the caravan station where the camps were pitched, and the pack-mules, ponies, and coolies driven in from China were relieved of their loads. They bring in tea, raw silk, walnuts, hides, gold, straw hats, and orpiment or king's yellow, the lemon-coloured tri-sulphide of arsenic used in dyeing and making yellow "lacquer." Sometimes the hardy little ponies are sold in Burma, but more often they go back to China laden with dry fish, cotton yarns and fabrics, or woollens. The trans-frontier trade with China is valued at close on £2,500,000 per annum.

The road from the caravan station along the river bank is called Irawadi Road up to the point where it is intersected at right angles by Ghat Road, running east from the ghat, beyond which it is called Chinese Bazaar. Turning down Ghat Road you come to the police station, two miles from where we left the steamer, and in front of the police station is a gilt Buddha.

The dak bungalow, the two forts, one to the east the other to the north, and the station where the caravan merchants from China must leave their arms on arrival at Bhamo, are all near this centre; but more interesting than all of these is the crowd to be seen in the Chinese Bazaar. There you may see warlike Chins from the western mountains, clothed only in a tiny loin-cloth, and wearing as ornaments curious necklaces and ear-rings, armed with bows and arrows, and carrying a small wicker basket slung by a basket-work strap across the shoulder, and perhaps a knife. Some of the men have their hair done up in a conical top-knot decorated with a long feather.

The Shan-Talok women have a useful piece of finery in the shape of a large, soft, straw hat, which falls gracefully over the shoulders and is decorated with bunches of straw ribbons. The Kachin women

Photographed by W. W. Schumacher.

CHINESE SHOP, BHAMO.

from the north wear a jacket and a *tamein*, or simple cloth folded over in place of a skirt, and carry heavy loads on their backs in baskets supported by a wicker strap coming over the head. They are very fond of decorating their clothes with cowries, and have cylinders of bamboo or amber an inch thick passing through the lobes of their ears. The Kachins from the hills bordering on China usually wear brown turbans, and the men are frequently seen, with a cheroot or roll of paper stuck over the left ear, carrying a huge knife (*dha*) in a rough sheath, and a big straw umbrella-hat slung over the back. Then there are the flat-nosed and fair-skinned Shan women, from the district to the east of Bhamo, dressed in black skirts with blue belts laced over them, white jackets, and on their heads black turbans folded in the shape of a high Parsi hat, sloping sharply backward from the forehead.

Chinese in their characteristic garb are everywhere, and representatives of many other races and tribes may be seen in Bhamo, but the most unique costume we saw was that worn by the Palaung women from Nam Hsan, east of Mogok. These women wore large cloth turbans, single-breasted jackets trimmed with cowries and beads, ornamented tameins, and trousers or puttees. Most of them carried a decorated bag hanging from the shoulder, and some wore ear-cylinders like those of the Kachin women, but their peculiar ornaments consist of a bone ring for a necklace and any number of wire rings around the body. Of the latter two or three are usually threaded with cowries. Similar rings are said to be worn by Kachin women. Many of these various tribes may be seen on the bazaar boats, which ply up and down the Irawadi carrying retail dealers and their wares from station to station.

The journey down from Bhamo, pronounced by Europeans as it is written, but by some of the natives called "Baamboo," is a very interesting one, and you are made very comfortable on the Flotilla steamers. The distances from station to station as well as the time occupied vary with the amount of water in the river, for even as high up as Myitkyina there is a difference of forty feet between low water and flood. During the times of flood a straight course can be steered up or down, while in low water the windings of the tortuous and shifting channel must be followed. The Flotilla Company have men constantly at work observing the changes in the river, and marking the navigable channel with bamboo poles tied to sand bags. These poles are painted white or red; and going down stream the red poles are kept to port and the white to starboard.

When you are stopping at a station the inhabitants will afford the greatest interest and amusement; but there are queer craft to be seen all along the river, birds of many kinds, dolphins of sorts which follow the boat and jump out of the river like porpoises, and queer fishing appliances. The latter take the form of big nets on bamboo frames hinged to a boat and moved in and out of the water by long bamboo levers.

The native boats are mostly dug-outs (*loung-goh*) fashioned from a single log of teak. To this single log plank sides are sometimes added to increase the freeboard, and the boat is then called a loung-sat, and sometimes they are built high at the bow and stern like the proper Burmese rice-boats (*hnaw*). The Shans take two dug-outs, build a platform over them, and so make a catamaran which is propelled with a paddle or punted with a pole. Then there are big rafts of teak logs floating down the river, some with as many as four cabins built on them, and we were informed that the Bombay and Burma Trading Company had at the time nearly fifty thousand logs on the Irawadi, worth from £5 to £7 each. In the season of 1902-3, the teak extracted from the Burmese forests was valued at £825,000.

The most common bird on the river is the snake-bird, a diving bird with black plumage and a long snake-like neck and head. It usually swims with its body submerged, showing only the neck and head above the surface. Then we saw orioles, orange-breasted pigeons, cranes in the water, and big herons in the trees, white-breasted kingfishers, birds of a similar appearance with blue wing-feathers and back and a black breast, black wading birds with white breasts and white tips to their wings, a bird having a red head with a black comb and a body with black and white stripes, and many species of the hawk tribe.

If there are any steam launches at Bhamo it is possible to run up through the first defile and

Photographed by Watts & Skeen.

ANGEL ROCK, SECOND IRAWADI DEFILE.

back during the day, and we were told that this defile is the finest of the three. The second defile is certainly not as fine as the Rhine or the Moselle, to say nothing of the Hudson; and the third defile is very much like the Thames at Cliveden.

Bhamo is 1028 miles from Rangoon by the river, according to the distances given by the Flotilla Company. Thirty miles down the river is Sawadi (Kaung Taung), and between this place and Sinkan, 13 miles below, is the second defile. Approaching this the first view is similar to that seen coming down the Thames when the Quarry Woods are seen rising behind Bisham. Then a bold cliff, 800 feet high, with almost perpendicular sides, appears to the right, its top covered with trees, and here the river narrows to little more than a hundred yards. Perched on a small hill at the foot of the cliff is a tiny pagoda, looking very fresh and bright in its framing of green trees. The majestic river flows swiftly between its rock-bound banks in the heart of a wilderness where modern progress is now represented by the steamer which hurries down the stream, and the telegraph wires spanning the river below from cliff to cliff. In half an hour we had passed the defile, and in another half hour the river had widened and shoaled so as to be again full of sand-banks.

We passed Sinkan, Shwegu, and Moda, and between the latter and Katha the Kaukkwe enters the Irawadi. We did the 110 miles from Bhamo to Katha in seven hours and a half. Lower down, near Kyetagaung, the Shweli enters from the east, and we tied up the first night at Tigyaing (Myadaung), 20 miles below Katha, four sailors springing overboard and swimming with the rope to the bank. The next morning we cast off at nine o'clock, and in two hours had done the 30 miles to Tagaung, a very ancient capital of these parts. An hour later the twin peaks of Shwe-nyaung-bin came into view 30 miles away to the south-east.

Twenty miles below Tagaung is Kyanhnyat, and it is another twenty miles to Male, near where the hills opposite come down to the river, and five miles more to Thabeikkyin, where we arrived at three o'clock. This is the landing for Mogok, the capital of the Ruby Mines district where the rubies and sapphires are found. Mogok lies up in the mountains thirty miles away as the crow flies. The metal cart-road is nearly sixty-two miles long, and there is a dak bungalow about every ten miles. But there are short cuts by bridle-paths, reducing the distance to about fifty miles, so that the journey can be easily done by pony in two days.

Below Thabeikkyin the river narrows and the hills close in on both sides, and half way to Kabwet, twenty-five miles from Thabeikkyin, the third (or, as some call it, the first) defile is entered. Mau is only five miles below Kabwet, and Kyaukmyaung ten miles further down, and we cast anchor the second evening about seven o'clock at a village near the latter place. The steamer carried a search-light, and the boys at the landing took a huge delight in stripping themselves and dancing about naked in its rays. The Tamil boys in Southern India played similar pranks, with the addition of indecent gestures, as we passed them on the railway.

The next morning we passed Ngasingu 250 miles from Bhamo, Sheinmaga 25 miles below, and 35 miles more brought us opposite Mingon.

To the north is a white pagoda with trees growing on it, then comes the great bell, in size second only to the one in the Kremlin (which weighs about 200 tons) hung on big timbers resting on brick piers, and supported on stones inserted below the lip which measures over 16 feet in diameter. The bell is nearly 12 feet high, 6 to 12 inches thick, and weighs 80 to 90 tons. South of the bell is the unfinished pagoda, a mass of solid brickwork 165 feet high and 230 feet square, split from top to bottom by the earthquake of 1839 and torn by thunderbolts, one corner entirely gone and the rest fallen to ruins. It stands on a platform 450 feet square, and there are over 8,000,000 cubic feet of bricks in this unfinished temple, which was begun by King Bo-daw-paya in the closing years of the eighteenth century. South of the temple on the river bank is the white Sibyo pagoda, with a porch in front and steps down to the water's edge.

We left the steamer at Mandalay, but one can go all the way from there to Rangoon by the Flotilla, a distance of 708 miles, stopping 120 miles down at Nyaungu, noted for its fine basket-wares covered with so-called lacquer, which is really made

Photographed by Watts & Skeen.

THE GREAT BELL AT MINGON.

of a sort of gum known as thitsi. Nyaungu is the landing-place for the celebrated ruins of Pagan, which was founded in the middle of the ninth century and was the capital seven hundred years ago, but was destroyed by the invading hordes of Kublai Khan in the year 1284. Lower down the river are the oil-wells at Yenangyat and at Yenangyaung. The former town is on the west bank 163 miles below Mandalay, and the latter is on the east bank 250 miles from Mandalay.

Crude petroleum has been known in Burma for over two thousand years, but it is only during the last ten years that its production has become of international importance. In 1796 Captain Cox estimated the output of the Yenangyaung wells at about 24,000,000 gallons. In 1902 the Burmese oil-fields yielded nearly 55,000,000 gallons, valued at the rate of 250 gallons for a sovereign, or less than a penny a gallon. The production in 1904 was 116,000,000 gallons of crude oil, of which over 73,000,000 gallons came from Yenangyaung. The steamer may be left at Prome, one of the most ancient of the many Burmese capitals, famous for its great Shwe-tsan-daw pagoda, and from Prome the railway may be taken to Rangoon 161 miles south-east.

NOTE TO CHAPTER V

Distances from Rangoon.	IRAWADI RIVER			Distances between stations.
	Rangoon	—	Prome	311 miles.
311	Prome	—	Yenangyaung	147 ,,
458	Yenangyaung	—	Yenangyat	87 ,,
545	Yenangyat	—	Nyaungu	43 ,,
588	Nyaungu	—	Mandalay	120 ,,
708	Mandalay	—	Mingon	10 ,,
718	Mingon	—	Sheinmaga	35 ,,
753	Sheinmaga	—	Ngasingu	25 ,,
778	Ngasingu	—	Kyaukmyaung	5 ,,
783	Kyaukmyaung	—	Mau	10 ,,
793	Mau	—	Kabwet	5 ,,
798	Kabwet	—	Thabeikkyin	25 ,,
823	Thabeikkyin	—	Male	5 ,,
828	Male	—	Kyanhnyat	20 ,,
848	Kyanhnyat	—	Tagaung	20 ,,
868	Tagaung	—	Tigyaing	30 ,,
898	Tigyaing	—	Katha	20 ,,
918	Katha	—	Moda	30 ,,
948	Moda	—	Shwegu	25 ,,
973	Shwegu	—	Sinkan	12 ,,
985	Sinkan	—	Sawadi	13 ,,
998	Sawadi	—	Bhamo	30 ,,
1028	Bhamo	—	Myitkyina	138 ,,
1166	Myitkyina	—	Rangoon	1166 miles.

CHAPTER VII

MANDALAY

The Queen's Golden Monastery—Fort Dufferin and the Royal Palace—"The centre of the universe"—King Thebaw and his Queens.

MANDALAY, founded in 1856, on the left bank of the Irawadi 315 feet above the sea, by Mindon Min, to-day spreads over an area measuring about six miles from north to south, and three miles from east to west. It is laid out on a grand scale, with "streets" running north and south, and "roads" running east and west, and boasts a double-track electric tramway six miles long. Near the middle of the city is Fort Dufferin, which was formerly called "the city," and in the centre of the fort stands the Royal Palace. The most westerly thoroughfare is the Strand Road on the bank of the river, about two miles from the palace. After leaving the steamer we drove up this road to 35th, or A, Road; crossed 84th, or Payagyi, Street; 83rd, or Merchant, Street; and turned up 80th, or West Moat, Street to the entrance of the fort.

The east and west roads from 22nd Road to 30th Road have the following alternative names:—C Road, Sladen Road, Convent Road, Telegraph Road, B Road (which skirts the south moat of the fort), Browning Road, Cooke Road, Fire Station Road, and Court House Road. In 36th Road, on the way to the fort, we visited the Queen's Golden Monastery, remarkable for its carved teak railings and roofs, erected by Thebaw's Queen, Supayalat, in the early eighties in honour of her mother Queen Shinbome, queen during five successive reigns. There is an instance in former times of a Burmese queen who was the consort of four of the royal line, and these facts may be adduced as convincing proof of the surpassing charm or exceeding cleverness of the women of Burma. Queen Shinbome, also called the Sin-byoo-me, the Sinpyumashin, or the Laungshe princess, was Mindon Min's chief queen and the mother of Supayagyi "the great princess," Supayalat "the middle princess," and

Photographed by Watts & Skeen.

WATCH TOWER, MANDALAY FORT.

Supayagale "the little princess." When Mindon died Shinbome shaped the course of events which brought Thebaw to the throne, and it was intended that Thebaw should marry all three of his half-sisters, and that Supayagyi should be the chief queen. But Supayalat captured Thebaw from the first, although in accordance with custom he married Supayagyi two years later, and Supayalat remained his only real wife to the end.

The crenelated brick walls of the fort, which enclose an area about 1¼ miles square, are surrounded by a broad moat, and crossing this by the bridge facing C Road, we entered the brick gateway and drove through avenues of tamarind trees to the Upper Burma Club located in the Royal Palace. Facing the entrance to the Club which is at the top of a handsome flight of thirteen steps, is a cannon built up of bars encircled by bands and having originally ten rings by which it could be carried. Behind the club, whose dining-room, which was the audience-room of the Queen, contains the Lily Throne, is the Great Hall of Audience with its Lion Throne, now used as a church. Since the Viceroy's visit to Mandalay, orders have been issued to move the club and the church to other quarters, and to restore the palace to its former condition.

Lord Curzon has earned the gratitude of all travellers and students by his efforts to restore and preserve relics of bygone times in India, and they will most heartily agree with the address from the managing committee of the Bombay branch of the Royal Asiatic Society, tendering their "sincere thanks for all His Excellency has done for the cause of Indian archæology, and more especially for the unremitting attention he has paid to the conservation of India's ancient monuments, culminating in the much desired Act for their effectual preservation."

Mandalay society was agitated at the time of our visit by a circular relating to the Burmese "wives" of government officials, and by the tragedy in Fort Dufferin on the 13th of December, when a Punjabi havildar (or sergeant) shot and killed a British captain and two native officers. After these murders he succeeded in passing the fort gates with his rifle, and in getting out of Mandalay. He was run down a few miles outside

Photographed by Watts & Skeen.

THE SUMMER-HOUSE WHERE KING THEBAW SURRENDERED.

the city, but committed suicide before he was captured.

The seven-roofed spire, or Shwepyathat, called by the natives "the centre of the universe," rises above the Lion Throne. Near this is the Nan-Myin, or watch-tower, ascended by an outside spiral staircase of seven cement and 153 wooden steps, to a platform, 78 feet above the ground, from which an excellent view over Mandalay and the surrounding country can be had. A little to the east of north is seen Mandalay Hill, rising to a height of 954 feet above the sea. In the opposite direction, south-by-east, is the Arakan pagoda near Shanzu station. To the south-west is the railway station, farther away are the carved roofs of the Queen's Golden Monastery, and the pagodas of Sagaing appear on the horizon beyond. South-west-by-south may be seen the steeple of a church—which the guide said was the Roman Catholic Cathedral—and in the distant south-west is a peak of the Shan hills.

The various structures of the royal palace are all built of wood, as indeed were all Burmese buildings except the pagodas; and owing to the perishable nature of the materials used little remains of this ancient architecture, but the forms of it are here preserved, although the palace, or nandaw, itself is quite modern. The flame-shaped ornamentations of the eaves, the seven-roofed tower, and the teak carvings are the distinctive features of Burmese wooden architecture. The carving is in many cases beautifully done, and is almost always bold and full of spirit. But it is too frequently marred by coatings of gaudy colours, and even the gorgeousness of new gold-leaf is small compensation for the loss of sharpness. It is no doubt true that the Burman can carve as well to-day as ever before, but the new carvings to be seen are generally only servile copies of the old designs without improvement or even refinement.

Some of the teak pillars in the Royal Palace are fully sixty feet high, and the overhanging eaves of the Lion Throne room are supported by newly gilded round timbers, inclined from the base of the building to the outer end of the eaves in the manner of posts holding out an awning. Close to the watch-tower is the theatre, and south of the latter a swimming-tank. Near this is the summer-

Photographed by W. W. Schumacher.

MINDON'S TOMB, MANDALAY FORT.

house, on the veranda of which is a brass plate with the following legend :—"King Theebaw sat at this opening with his two Queens and the Queen Mother when he gave himself up to General Prendergast on November 30, 1885." The "Queen Mother" was the masterful Shinbome, and "his two Queens" the neglected Supayagyi and the jealous Supayalat, who tyrannised the weak Thebaw to the end.

Within the fort on the East Palace Road near the East Gate Road is the tomb of Maung Lwin, Mindon Min, the father and predecessor of Thebaw. The mausoleum is square with a seven-storied pyramidal roof in a perfect state of preservation, every detail being intact, and the gilding as bright as when first put on. It is on a white platform, having a rail with an opening in the centre of each face approached by a flight of six steps, and the whole has been enclosed with an iron railing to preserve it. Near it are other royal tombs, including the tomb of Mindon's favourite queen, and not far away is the monastery, with its elaborately carved roofs, where Burma's last king was educated. There is also a massive bell-tower ; but without a bell.

CHAPTER VIII

MANDALAY—(*continued*)

Sermons in stones—The Eindawya pagoda—The game of chinlon—A Burmese pwe—The Great Temple and the Mahamani.

OUTSIDE of Fort Dufferin near the east gate is the fine old Taikdaw monastery, whose carvings have gone to ruin and whose basements shelter litters of pigs and flocks of rabbit-eared goats. Near the base of Mandalay Hill, around which there is a drive, and to the top of which there is more than one ceremonial road, is the enclosure of the Kuthodaw, or "Charity" pagoda built by Thebaw's uncle. The southern entrance has well-carved teak gates, the central pagoda is 100 feet high, and on the platform was an old boat. Around the central pagoda are arranged 729 square pavilions, under each of which is an upright slab, like a tombstone, carved from top to bottom with black letters. On one side of each slab part of the Buddhist scriptures is carved in Burmese characters and on the other side in Pali. Here, indeed, might the pongyis repeat the lines spoken in the Forest of Arden :—

> " And this our life, exempt from public haunt
> Finds tongues in trees, books in the running brooks,
> Sermons in stones and good in every thing."

South of the Kuthodaw stood the Incomparable Monastery destroyed by fire in 1892, and east of the latter is the Glass Monastery. To the west of the Kuthodaw are the buildings of the Royal Monastery, and west of Fort Dufferin is the Thathanabaing Kyoung.

The Eindawya pagoda is south of B Road and west of 85th Street not far from the Zegyo Bazaar, the solidly built new Municipal Markets replacing the old one burnt in 1897. The Eindawya, built in 1847 by Pagan Min, is one of the most magnificent pagodas in Burma. It is entirely gilt from base to top, and so richly and heavily covered with gold-leaf as to appear to be solid gold. It has a square base, built in three terraces having a lion-like monster at each corner, and a staircase to the third terrace up the centre of each side. The base of the pagoda is surrounded by an iron railing, and the shrines and monasteries are relegated to the outer side of the wide platform, so that there is an unobstructed view of the whole pagoda from base to ti. On the west side is the Mahuya Paya brought here from Gaya in 1839.

The pagoda platform is a favourite place to hold a grand pwe, and it is also a great resort for the experts in Burmese football or chinlon, a sort of battledore and shuttlecock played with a hollow wicker sphere and the feet. The ball is thrown in the air and allowed to fall behind the back of the player, who catches it on the heel or the sole of the foot before it reaches the ground, and kicks it straight up into the air. The ball may be caught in front on the knee or toes, but the back strokes are more favoured. There are no sides, but the players stand around near each other, and the one who first fails to send the ball up in the air falls out. As an exhibition of skill the game is very interesting, and as an exhibition of masculine grace there is nothing, except skating, with which it can be compared.

Photographed by Watts & Skeen.

THE GAME OF CHINLON.

(The "ball" is in the air, to the right of the player's head.)

The pwe is the great national amusement of the Burmese, and the zat-pwe its most common form. On moonlight nights, and particularly when there is a full moon, you may hear the beating of the drums, and guided by the sound can make your way to the show. It may be held in any open space, such as a temple platform, or it may be in a specially constructed building, having a proper elevated stage lit by a row of oil lamps hanging in front at about the level of the performers' heads, a curtain displaying the Palace Gates, Mandalay, and steps at the sides. The auditorium is a lofty wooden shed, whose roof is supported by posts and whose floor is beaten earth. In front of the stage, seated on the ground, is the orchestra. The instruments are the big drum, suspended to an ornamental support; the *seing-weing*, a series of small drums arranged around the interior of a low cylinder in the centre of which the musician sits; the *kyi-weing*, a similar arrangement of bells or gongs; split-bamboo clappers, or *wah-lekhoht*, worked by a number of performers; a wooden pipe or wind instrument called a *nhae*, which makes harsh sounds "slightly resembling an air," and seems to call the tune; and flutes (*puloay*), one of which the leader blows.

The Burman comes with his whole family and their bedding; and, if he is a connoisseur, before paying to see the show, he mounts the steps to the stage, goes behind the scenes, inspects the performers and their state of preparedness, and, if satisfied, pays the entrance money, spreads his mats on the ground, and perhaps goes to sleep until the performance begins, and may do the same during the dull parts and intermissions.

The drums begin to play early in the evening, but the usual hours for the performances are from 11 P.M. to sunrise, with the choice bits coming on about one o'clock. The curtain rises on the princess, who gives a dance which will be short if the audience is small, and longer if there are special visitors or the audience is large. She is dressed in a tight-fitting, trailing *lungyi*, which is sewn on and allows of little movement of the legs, although it is open at one side almost to the knee. The bodice is a flesh-coloured *tricot*, with sleeves and fan-shaped pieces hanging at the back and at each side. She wears a number of necklaces, generally strings of

Photographed by Watts & Skeen.

MUSICIANS AND DANCERS, BURMESE PWE.

beads, which hang down to the waist in front, and carries a handkerchief. The dance consists of swayings of the body from the waist, expandings of the chest, stampings of the feet, and rapid changes of the arms and hands from one constrained angular position to another. After the curtain rings down on the dance, King Thebaw and his ministers file slowly across the stage before the curtain. The higher the performer stands in the profession the more slowly he goes across; the leading man advancing by almost imperceptible movements and taking some minutes to cross over. Then the curtain rises on the king and his ministers, and if you don't understand their conversation, which may last an hour or two, you go home, and if you do understand it, you blush.

More interesting are the temple yein-pwes, given in the open air on the pagoda platforms where the crowd is greater, the dancers more numerous, and the moonlight effects more picturesque; but most interesting are the pwes given at the funeral of a monk (*pongyi-byan*), where gigantic wood and paper animals attend the funeral car. In the country, the neighbouring villages take turns in entertaining each other at their pwes, and in the bigger places, like Mandalay, the various districts hold their temple pwes in well-regulated succession. Another form of pwe is the *yoht-the* or marionette show.

The most venerated of the Mandalay pagodas is the square Arakan pagoda or Paya Gyi, the "Great Temple," built in seven stories diminishing in size and surmounted by a fine ti. Its base is surrounded by corridors, and has a chamber in each face. The main chamber contains the famous brass Gawdama, Mahamani, brought over the mountains from Arakan through the Taungup Pass in 1787 by King Bo-daw-paya (Mentara-gyi), after the successful campaign by the Crown Prince against that country in 1784, and first housed in a pagoda at Amarapura. It is a seated image 12 feet 7 inches high to the top of the magaik, or tiara, and although the Burmese are firmly convinced that the statue is contemporary with the Buddha himself, or at least not later than the sixth century B.C., there is no reason to doubt that it was cast in the second century of our era. It is heavily coated with gold-leaf, and you can buy one for a rupee, follow the

Photographed by W. W. Schumacher.

ARAKAN PAGODA AND TURTLE TANK.

pilgrims up the steps leading behind the image, and plaster the leaf on the Buddha's back.

In the north-west court are colossal bronze images, which the true believers treat in the same manner as the wooden images of the god Binzuru are treated in Japan. If you have a bad eye, rub the eye of the god and then your own, and so on. The curious will be able to judge what are the complaints most common in Mandalay, by noting the parts of these bronze images most worn away by repeated rubbings. Leading away from the Buddha is a colonnade, on one side of which hang two bells and on the other is the turtle tank, where you buy food for the turtles, and find it snapped up by the crows before the turtles get a chance at it. At the entrance facing the street are two colossal griffins, one of which was stencilled with the advertisement of an American sewing-machine, and the other plastered with small bills asking you to "Vote for Mg. Kanbaw." Maung (Mg.) means male or Mr.; Ma female or wife. There are numerous small pagodas near the Arakan, and close to the Shanzu station is a great mass of brickwork like the base of one unfinished.

Mandalay is famous for its hand-woven silk lungyis, which European ladies buy to make into petticoats. The silk is thin but does not crack, and is said to be improved by washing. The Bazaar, which is most crowded between six and eight o'clock in the morning, contains other attractions, and many interesting hours may be spent there.

Photographed by W. W. Schumacher.

ENTRANCE TO ARAKAN PAGODA, MANDALAY.

CHAPTER IX

GOKTEIK

The railway to Lashio—The Gokteik gorge and viaduct—The natural bridge—Maymyo—The excursion to Moulmein.

FROM Mandalay we went by way of Myohaung Junction, three miles south, to the famous Gokteik gorge and the viaduct over it. Immediately after Sedaw, thirteen miles from the junction, the line begins to ascend the precipitous mountain-side by a series of zig-zags. There are four reversing stations between Sedaw and Maymyo, a distance of twenty-six miles, and on some of the gradients, which are as steep as 1 in 25, sand tracks are arranged so that a runaway train or carriage would be brought to a standstill in troughs of sand. The first station after Sedaw is Zibingyi, 1857 feet above the sea, and on the way up Mandalay hill can be seen on a clear day almost due west. After Zibingyi come

Thondaung, 2700 feet above the sea, and Maymyo, 3481 feet above the sea, the highest point on the railway.

Double "Fairlie"-type engines are used to haul the trains, but we made very poor time to Maymyo, as the brake-blocks on some of the passenger carriages worked badly and forced the train to pull up more than once. From Maymyo (myo is Burmese for town) to Gokteik viaduct is forty miles, and the stations on the way with their elevations above the sea are Wetwun, 2775 feet; Hsum Hsai, 2437 feet; and Nawnghkio, 2723 feet. Before you arrive at Gokteik you go through a rock cutting, and on coming out of the cutting there is a good view of the viaduct and of the line on the other side of the gorge going up the face of the cliff and through two tunnels to the table-land above. But perhaps the best view of the viaduct is from the railway dak bungalow on the hill straight above it. To get a view of the gorge itself you can walk out on the viaduct, or take the train farther up the line and see it from the north cliffs.

The Gokteik gorge is in the North Shan States on a tributary of the Myit-nge, called the Nam Hpa

Photographed by the Author.

GOKTEIK VIADUCT—TRAIN APPROACHING.

Se, which is interrupted here by a great dyke running across the valley. Through this dyke, which is 500 feet high, and runs about north and south, the river has bored a tunnel or cave, 150 feet high at its opening up stream, but narrowing like a funnel, so converting the dyke into a natural bridge. The piers of the viaduct rest on the natural bridge, one of them being above the opening of the cave, and the rails are 320 feet higher, or 820 feet above the river, at the elevation of 2133 feet above the sea; while the cliffs on the side opposite the station rise several hundred feet higher. The chaukidar of the bungalow told us that it is 1360 feet from the top of the viaduct to the river, which he called the Chaungzon; but, like most native information, his is not to be relied upon.

The viaduct is 1620 feet long, and was built by the Pennsylvania Steel Company. Work was begun on January 9, 1900, and the viaduct was completed and trains run over it on June 1, 1901. This was accomplished by transporting to the spot the most approved labour-saving machines, as well as expert artisans capable of working them to the best advantage. Although its rapid construction was a great engineering feat, the viaduct does not add to the natural beauties of the scene. To visit the river cave you should wear heavy boots, and if you penetrate into the cave you must not be afraid of a wetting. A long overcoat or a skirt is sure to come out with wet tails. There is a waterfall like a shower-bath that you must pass through, after entering the cave from whose walls hang small stalactites; the rock floor of the cavern is worn into curious swirls by the action of the river; and there is a curve in its course underground, so that you cannot see the entrance up stream when you get to the point where daylight shows through the smaller opening at the farther end.

You can go down from the dak bungalow to the far end of the cave and back in an hour and a half, and in another half hour walk across the top of the natural bridge by the rough path at the side of the viaduct piers.

There is fine scenery on the way to Lashio, the present terminus of the line, ninety-seven miles beyond Gokteik and 3100 feet above the sea. The road was completed in 1903 to Lashio, from which it is ninety-five miles by a fair road to Kunlong

Photographed by Watts & Skeen.

ENTRANCE OF CAVE—GOKTEIK VIADUCT.

Ferry over the Salwin into China. From the district to the west of the railway comes hlapet or "pickled tea," the anti-soporific so largely used by the pwe-going Burmese. Between Se-En and Manpwe stations are fine waterfalls, close under which the railway runs before it mounts the hill by their side. At Baudwen, about forty-five miles from Hsipaw station, are some old mines, formerly worked by the Chinese for silver. The large percentage of lead in the ore was disregarded as being too heavy to transport at a profit. Since the railway has been built it has become possible to work the old tailings for the lead, and the Burma Mines, Railway, and Smelting Company was formed in March, 1906, to take over the mines.

When we were at Gokteik there was only one train a day to return by, and this train only ran as far as Maymyo, so that we could only travel forty-one miles by rail during the whole day; and this made it necessary to expend three days and two nights over the round trip from Mandalay, when it could have been comfortably done in two days and a night, or possibly in twenty-four hours. An accelerated express service would be much appreciated by many tourists, who would then be less likely to miss a chance of seeing the finest bit of scenery on the Burma railways. The railway has shown an enlightened liberality in erecting a comfortable dak bungalow at Gokteik, which can be occupied free of charge; but there is no food to be had there unless you give a day's notice to the manager of the refreshment room at Maymyo, who will then make arrangements to provide meals.

Maymyo has a very fine new dak bungalow on Lodge Road, about a quarter of a mile from the station. The town is still only a straggling village, but it is rapidly growing, and is highly thought of as a sanatorium and hot-weather resort.

On Tuesdays, Thursdays, and Saturdays, steamers sail each way between Rangoon and Moulmein, and at six o'clock in the morning we cast off from the Mogul Street jetty for Moulmein, where we arrived at half-past four. The distance is 140 miles, and crossing the Gulf of Martaban you sight, on the Tenasserim coast, Double Island light and the Water pagoda off Amherst, the latter named after the Lord Amherst who was Governor-General of India when this coast, which extends south to

Victoria Point within ten degrees of the equator, was annexed. Entering the mouth of the Salwin, locally known as the Moulmein, river by the New Channel, the Kwang-la pagoda, 183 feet high, is seen four miles to the north of Amherst. Moulmein is nearly twenty-five miles from the first buoy in the entrance to the New Channel, and on the way up Long Island, Mupun Island (both in mid stream), and New Island, to the west of the channel, are passed. Just above Moulmein three rivers meet: the Salwin coming from the north, the Gyaing from the east, and the Attaran from the south-east. From Martaban, the old Talaing capital opposite Moulmein, the Darebank or Martaban river, really one of the mouths of the Salwin, runs west to the gulf, and forms with the Moulmein river the island of Balugyun. Between Moulmein and Martaban lies the small island of Goungzay-gyoun with its little pagoda.

CHAPTER X

MOULMEIN

The Duke's Head—The great Moulmein pagoda—The bells—Ivory carvers—Kado—A modern shrine.

THE Toung-ngyo hills, which form the backbone of Moulmein, are covered with green, crowned with pagodas, and fringed with shops and warehouses. The town itself looks very pretty from a distance, although in reality it is very dirty and shabby; and the pagodas are more picturesque as seen from the river than they are upon a closer inspection.

Of the Moulmein pagodas the most northerly is the Great Pagoda, south of this are Old Pagoda, Signal Pagoda with a flagstaff, and Uzina or South Pagoda, while to the south-west of these is Mupun Pagoda. The two largest pagodas show up well against the sky-line, and in the distant north, forty miles up the river, a mountain peak called the

"Duke of York's (some say Wellington's) Head," points to the heavens a profile showing with great distinctness the forehead, eyebrows, nose, mouth, double chin, and neck-cloth, all complete. On landing you find that the street running alongside the river is, as usual, called the Strand Road. The next street running parallel is Lower Main Street, the principal thoroughfare, and the next beyond it Upper Main Street.

The principal sights of Moulmein can be done in three hours. A gharry will take you up the road at the back of the Uzina pagoda, so that you reach the platform by the steps on the east side. Turning to the right to the north-east corner, there is a great Buddha's foot (Shwe-zet-daw) carved in stone, with a sculptured border of bulls and hans around it. The toes are all of equal length, and each is decorated with a spirally twisted conical shell, while the hollow of the foot bears the wheel of the law. The corners of the pagoda platform have figures with two bodies and only one head, and at the top of the north steps are images in the attitude of prayer. The shrine of the seated Buddha by the north base of the pagoda was being repainted, the shrine at the north-west base contains a gilded and glass-jewelled Buddha with a silk drapery, while the shrine at the south-west base covers a similar Buddha and four others standing in various attitudes, each with a chhatra over his head, as well as eight seated Buddhas and two kneeling elephants. On the southern edge of the platform is a pavilion covering a number of carved and painted wooden figures, some of them, such as the four beggars, being very fine indeed.

The Signal pagoda and the Old pagoda are uninteresting; but the Kyaikthanlan, or Great, pagoda, has more to offer to the curious, although the gilt on the pagoda itself and on the small pagodas and shrines surrounding its base is much tarnished and worn away. Mounting to the platform by the southern stairway and turning to the right, you come at the south-east corner to the famous bell hanging from a beam supported by four pillars. Around the bell is inscribed :—" This Bell is made by Koo Na Lin Gah Yah the priest and weight 600 viss. No one body design to destroy this Bell. Maulmain, March 30, 1855. He who destroyed to this Bell, they must be in

Photographed by Watts & Skeen.

THE BELL, MOULMEIN PAGODA.

the great Heell, and unable to coming out." In front of an adjoining shrine containing a brass Buddha is another bell bearing the following inscription on one side:—"Maulmain 6th March 1887 at 2 P.M. . . . cast a bell by the name of Madoothara made in the quiet reign of Queen Victoria. The dimensions 3 ft. 6 inches in diameter 4 ft. in height 10 ft. 6 inches in circumference 4 inches in thickness weight 1028 viss . . . do not destroy to this tremendous bell." You may, without danger of giving offence, ring the bell by striking it three times with a deer's horn lying by it—the usual way of ringing bells at Burmese temples.

At the top of the north stairs are seated human figures with elephant heads similar in form to the Hindu Ganesa, and the shrine close by contains a gilt seated Buddha with a standing image on each side. The shrine with a Chinese inscription on the doorway on the west side of the base of the pagoda shelters the largest Buddha, the shrine south of this has only a small brass Buddha, and the next one has a Buddha seated on a throne with a screen at the back, both the throne and screen inlaid with mirrors and coloured glass-work. A similar glass-work pedestal supports one reclining and six seated Buddhas in the shrine at the south end of the platform.

Perhaps the most satisfactory thing about Kyaikthanlan is the view from the sides of its platform. The ridge of hills runs due north and south, and the pagoda is built on the most northern eminence. To the east can be seen the Attaran river, and farther away to the north-east the Farm Cave hills. Part of Moulmein lies to the north and east of the pagoda, but most of the population live on the west slope of the ridge. The view on the north is bounded on the east side of the Salwin by the Zwekabin range, of which the Duke's Head is the most westerly peak, while to the west of the Salwin, north of Moulmein, are the Zingyaik hills. At the base of the pagoda to the north-west lies the jail, which contains nothing of interest, and across the river is Martaban. To the south is the line of pagodas and pongyi-kyoungs on the ridge, and to the south-west of them the Myangoon pagoda with curious images of tattooed *nats* guarding its entrance.

Photographed by the Author

KADO LANDING.

The ivory carvers in the Padeintan Quarter, Daingwunkwin, had little to show except mediocre paper-cutters and backs for hand-glasses. One of them, however, exhibited a pavilion about six inches high with a Buddha inside all carved out of a solid piece, for which he asked one hundred and fifty rupees; and a dancing girl or princess, wearing a seven-tiered skirt inlaid with precious stones, made to the order of a Rangoon official, which could be duplicated for two hundred and fifty rupees. The prices asked by the carvers for inferior work were ridiculously high, and the silversmiths showed nothing but coarse or damaged pieces. Yet we found on visiting Kado that as good work can be done by the Burmese artisans of to-day as has been done by their predecessors.

Leaving Kulladan Jetty near the north end of Lower Main Road, Moulmein, the Irawadi Flotilla Company's launch lands you at Kado in about an hour and a half. There is a picturesque but somewhat dilapidated landing-place, and following the street leading away from the river you take the first turning to the left and continue for less than a mile to the pagoda compound. On the way is passed the house of Maung Shwe Hla, the present head of the family to whom Kado owes its religous buildings and its consequent fame. The buildings were erected at the end of the last century, and the workmanship displayed, in reproducing the old forms as well as the elaboration of the details, is as good as can be seen anywhere in Burma.

To the right on entering the enclosure is a large building containing a hall with a ceiling of twelve coffers decorated with coloured glass and supported by eight pillars with capitals of glass mosaic. The shrine has before it a pair of curtains embroidered with peacocks in shwechido work of gold and silver thread and spangles. All this is in good (Burmese) taste, but the jarring modern note is simultaneously struck by over a dozen American "office clocks," all of the same pattern and make, which ornament the pillars and walls. To the north-east of this building is an octagonal pagoda with a gilded top. In front of the pagoda is the usual bell, and to the south of it is a building with an octagonal fore-porch and a connecting gallery decorated with paintings. Instead of a shrine is a large glass case

Photographed by the Author.

SHRINES ON NORTH SIDE OF KADO PAGODA.

containing eight carved tusks and a number of small ivory figures.

On the north of the pagoda is a group of three shrines in line east and west. The most westerly one has a gilt seven-roofed shrine, and a porch whose roof is supported by nineteen pillars arranged in three groups of three, and five of two each. The pillars are all inlaid with mirrors and coloured glass patterns, and around the inside of the porch there is a frieze of carved wooden figures in panels, while the ceiling is divided into four coffers. The shrine itself contains Buddhas in brass, wood, and marble, and before them on the floor stand some good wood carvings, including a couple of tattooed beggars, one seated and one standing, and three pairs of gong- or bell-holders. The roof of the shrine rests on six pillars, and light is admitted from above just at their tops under the eaves. When we visited Kado a pongyi had recently died, and his body, preserved in honey, had been encased in a coffin (*pyoung-bong*) shaped like a dragon with shining glass scales, and was lying in state in the centre of the porch.

The central building, which is oblong in plan, has

a floor of marble and encaustic tiles laid in squares, and a ceiling with nine coffers, also supported so as to admit light from under the eaves. The shrine has six pillars encrusted with glass, and contains two standing images of heroic size robed in gilt and jewelled gowns, while at their feet kneel three worshippers, also in gilt and jewelled robes. This group is supposed to represent Maung Shwe Hla and his father and uncle, the builders of the shrines, and their tutelary deities.

The easternmost shrine contains a brass Buddha seated on a pedestal of coloured glass mosaic before a background of glass and gold. To the north of these three shrines is a pongyi-kyoung, and scattered about the grounds are dwelling-places and other conveniences for the priests and caretakers of the temple.

CHAPTER XI

CHRISTMAS IN BURMA

Christmas Eve smoking concert—Christmas at the Farm Caves —Rangoon to Chittagong—New Year's Day at Akyab.

THE sights of Moulmein and Kado were seen on Boxing Day. On Christmas Eve we were invited to the Amateur Smoking Concert at Moulmein Gymkhana Hall, where the microcosm of Moulmein society could be seen in its entirety, for the audience and the singers represented every branch of the business and social life of Moulmein. Social lines are less rigidly drawn here than in India "proper," and Europeans, Eurasians, and Asiatics mix pretty freely in these functions. The government, the great trading companies, the shipping interests, finance, the law, the medical profession, the army, and the visitors had all at least one representative on the programme. It was only near the end that the audience warmed up and entered heart and lungs into the choruses, but enthusiastic applause and shouts of "En-caw, caw, caw," greeted the end of "There were Three Crows," after which we rose to sing "God Save the King," before adjourning to the bar for a stirrup-cup and the exchange of hearty wishes for "A Merry Christmas." Then we arranged a picnic for the following day to the Farm Caves, and went back to our bunks on board ship.

We were awakened from sweet dreams by the flash of a lantern and a sharp command from a strange voice to "Get up, mister, and come out!" In answer to our dazed "Who are you?" the reply came, "Father Christmas, don't delay." So we crawled out from under the mosquito-nets, and went on deck in pyjamas to find "all hands forward to splice the main brace." The captain's health was duly drunk in champagne with musical honours, some other pleasant compliments of the season passed, and when we again retired to our cabins it was "Some wee short hour ayont the twal."

Christmas morning opened in brilliant sunshine, and after breakfast we started for the Farm or

Photographed by the Author.

MOULMEIN HACKNEY CARRIAGE.

Ka-yon Caves. The English name is supposed to have been derived from the Shan word Pharum. Ka-yon is the Burmese name. There were eight of us, three-fourths being undoubted Scots from whom we gathered that India had been mainly colonised from Scotland, and was now chiefly managed by the abilities and for the benefit of North Britain. We spent a full eight-hour day on our picnic away from the ship, but as an excursion it could be done in a couple of hours less. First we drove about four miles—to Nioungbenziak, where there is a ferry over the Attaran river—in gharries, and the Moulmein gharries are perhaps the cheapest hackney carriages in the world. The legal fare by day is three annas the first mile and two annas for each mile after the first, or eight annas for the first hour and six for each succeeding hour. By the half day of five hours the fare is twenty-four annas, and by the day of ten hours, forty annas. Think of a legal fare of three shillings and fourpence without tips for a ten-hour day! There are even cheaper cabs for poor folk and better ones, they say, but we saw none of the latter; and we were quite prepared to believe that living is cheap in Moulmein.

At the village on the farther bank of the Attaran we found the ox-carts, which we had engaged by messenger the previous evening, and started on a jolting drive of an hour and a half, along a road lined for the most part with palm trees, to the entrance of the first cave. The road runs eastward as a dyke, across flat fields, from a hill with three pagodas to the range of knife-edge rocks, rising precipitously from the plains, in which the caves are found, and there was a bad break in this dyke between the $6\frac{1}{4}$ and $6\frac{1}{2}$ milestones. Except for this short distance the road was quite good enough for bicycling, and the four miles or so from the ferry could be easily done in thirty-five minutes.

The Attaran river is in sight to the south, and just beyond the $8\frac{1}{2}$ milestone from Moulmein a road branches off to the south from the main road, crosses a little nullah by a bridge and leads to the caves. The knife-edge range runs north-west to south-east, and on the most northern point is a small pagoda reached from the east side by a series of ladders up the face of the cliffs. The entrance to the first cave is approached by a flight of steps

Photographed by the Author.

CHRISTMAS LUNCH WITH THE BUDDHAS, FARM CAVES.

leading to a platform on which stands a small pagoda, and at the right-hand side of the pagoda is a gallery, running along the side of the cliff, containing many gigantic Gawdamas, as well as another pagoda. The cave itself runs almost due north into the cliffs, and its mouth has a small dome carved out of the rock above, lined with concentric circles of tiny Gawdamas, while throughout the entire length of the cave are two rows of sitting and recumbent Buddhas. An opening in the left-hand row leads into a lofty cave, lit from above by an opening in the cliff, and at the far end of this cave is a ladder about ten feet long up to a sort of cave or tunnel into the rock.

After having discussed the contents of our tiffin baskets, presided over by the only lady of the party, and made great inroads, notwithstanding her protests, into the store of liquid refreshments, we sang "Auld Lang Syne," and then it was discovered that none of the Scots knew that the last line of the first verse reads "And days o' lang syne?" whereas the first line of the refrain is "For auld lang syne, my dear." The poet of the party composed the following parody:—

By the old Moulmein pagoda,
  Looking westward to the sea,
There are Burmese girls a plenty,
  But they have no charm for me.
Though the temple bells keep ringing,
  Yet they only seem to say :—
Your own kind are for all time,
  And these but for a day.
    On the road to Mandalay,
    Which is quite another way,
    You'll get very hot and dusty
    From Rangoon by train all day.

Ship me somewhere west of Suez,
  Where my mother-tongue is spoke ;
And they raise an awful rumpus
  At each commandment broke ;
Where the food is clean and tasty,
  Where the bedding is all right,
Where the water's pure and wholesome,
  And your sweetheart's skin is white,
    Which it ain't in Mandalay,
    Where you buy a wife and pay
    By agreement with her mother
    In the usual Burmese way.

After making a careful examination of the cave, we walked about half a mile by a rough cart-road to the Sad-dan cave. The entrance to this cave, or rather series of caves, is much higher up the face of the cliff. In addition to the entrance, which is approached by steep steps and which faces nearly east, there is another opening facing north-east,

Photographed by the Author.

"THE ONLY LADY OF THE PARTY."

which is screened by a tattered curtain of rock, and serves as a window to light the large cave. The main trend of the underground galleries is here north and south. We thoroughly explored these galleries, following each ramification until it got too small to proceed farther, and lighting up the vaults far above with magnesium lights and rockets, to the infinite disgust of the birds and the wild terror of the bats who flew overhead in thousands. The caves were quite dry and free from damp in almost every part, and are decorated throughout with stalactites, stalagmites, "rock-falls," and in places with huge roots of trees, which have pierced the roofs of the caves and come straight down through the air to strike into the floors.

As we came from the ferry in the morning, we noticed by the side of the road the carcase of a cow just dead, and saw the vultures gathering for the feast; on our return four hours later only the big rib bones, picked clean, were left. A solitary grey adjutant stork with white legs and fawn-coloured feet, and a neck almost as bare as those of the vultures, seemed to have been assisting them. The adjutant is a bird as tall as a man, and the under-feathers of the wings and tail are the marabou feathers of commerce.

While waiting for the ferry, we watched a party of small boys playing marbles for pice, and found they were well provided with these copper coins. The marble is held between the tips of the thumb and the forefinger of the right hand, and shot out with the middle finger of the left hand. We returned to the boat for a Christmas dinner of roast turkey, plum-pudding, and mince pies, and finished up with a water-melon, which only faintly recalled the flavour of the American variety. The thermometer in the cabin registered 90° during the day, and this was the highest point it reached during our tour in India.

From Moulmein we returned to Rangoon, and at Rangoon took the coasting steamer for Chittagong. Most tourists would be well advised to go direct from Rangoon to Calcutta, even if they intend to visit friends in Assam, as some days are lost in making the voyage up the Arakan coast, and the railway into the country from Chittagong is inconvenient and slow.

However, we left Rangoon on December 28,

1904, at 6 A.M., passed Elephant Point at 8.30, and at 9.45 were between the China Bakir light and the pilot brig *Kyauktan*. At 4.15 P.M. the cherub log registered 71 miles from the brig, and we were opposite the Baragua lightship, and five hours later, 128 miles from the brig, we had the Alguada light abeam.

Alguada light is off Cape Negrais, which is north of Pagoda Point, the south-west point of Lower Burma and of the Arakan coast, which latter extends north to the Naf estuary at Chittagong. The next day at noon we had steamed 190 miles from Alguada light, and had just passed the volcanic Foul Island, recently surveyed for a lighthouse. At 2.15 P.M. we cast anchor in the open roadstead of Sandoway, the Burmese Thandwe, where we remained less than an hour and a half. About 8 P.M. we were off the south-western point of Cheduba Island, and the next morning anchored in Kyaukpyu harbour at the northern end of Ramri Island, where we remained less than two hours. The same day, at 4 P.M., two hours after passing a gold-tipped pagoda on the coast, we made fast to the wharf at Akyab.

Akyab, situated on an island, is the third port in Burma, ranking after Rangoon and Moulmein. The distances logged between Sandoway and Kyaukpyu vary, according to whether the "inside" or "outside" course is taken, from 88 to 143 miles. But from Rangoon to Sandoway is 364 miles, and from Kyaukpyu to Akyab 88 miles; while from Akyab to Chittagong is 194 miles, and from Chittagong to Calcutta 378 miles.

The harbour of Akyab is protected by a line of reefs, on which is placed the Savage Island lighthouse, and is entered by a narrow channel. The scenery is very pretty, the fishing-boats with matting sails very quaint, and the natives have the Chinese custom of painting eyes on their sampans. The ancient capital of Arakan, Myohaung, lies fifty miles to the north-east on the Kaladan river. Akyab boasts a club, a clock-tower, a racecourse, and since 1877 a municipal bazaar. There you can spend hours watching the people in their various occupations and affairs.

We left Akyab harbour about noon on Monday, January 2, 1905, and after steaming twenty-nine miles had Oyster Rock light abeam. The next

Photographed by the Author.

BARGE ON ARAKAN COAST.

morning, about nine, we anchored at the mouth of the Chittagong (or Karnaphuli) river. The buildings on the hills in Chittagong, the ancient Islamabad, can be seen from the anchorage, but it is difficult to make out the river's mouth, even when it is only a couple of miles away. This coast was visited by a cyclone, October 24, 1897, which caused the loss of 14,000 lives. We waited at the anchorage until noon, when we started and picked up our moorings, about 12 or 14 miles up the river, opposite the town, an hour and a half later.

CHAPTER XII

ASSAM

Chittagong—The Assam-Bengal railway—Big game—The planters—The romance of Assam—The tea industry

THE most prominent buildings in Chittagong are the offices of the Assam-Bengal Railway, on the top of one hill; and, on the top of another, the post-office, circuit-court, and dak bungalow, all under one roof. Chittagong presents no special feature of interest; but it is the headquarters of the race of lying, quarrelsome, Moslem boatmen and longshoremen employed in the Bay of Bengal, along its coasts, and up the rivers emptying into it, as the Lascars are similarly employed in the Arabian Sea. There are no European books on sale in Chittagong, nor any newspapers: and it appears that the ticket-seller at the railway station does not even read his company's time-tables, as he said he had never heard of, or sold a ticket to, Kamarbandha Ali, a station 460 miles from Chittagong up the main line.

The Assam-Bengal railway is a metre-gauge line open from Chittagong to Tinsukia in the Brahmaputra valley, a distance of 574 miles, with branches aggregating about 165 miles in length. In addition to the very exceptional damage, amounting to over £90,000, it received in the earthquake of June 12, 1897, when over 1500 people were killed in Assam, the railway is subject to annual damage during the rains in the difficult hill section, and elsewhere on the line. For it must be remembered that one place in the Khasi Hills north-west of the railway holds the world's record for rainfall, and after the rains trains are liable to interruptions, even if the line is not in places entirely carried away, and constant labour is required to keep the line in working condition.

The closest connection we could make involved a wait of eight hours at Laksam Junction, so we took the train down to Chandpur on the east bank of the Meghna, one of the great rivers formed by the junction of the Ganges and the Brahmaputra.

There we waited for the Calcutta mail, which comes down by steamer from Goalundo, and had our dinner in the restaurant-car on the way back to Laksam. During the night we skirted the western and northern borders of Hill Tippera, and the next day was spent in traversing the hill section between Badarpur, the junction for the Silchar branch, and Lumding, the junction for Gauhati. After crossing the Surma river the line goes up the Jatinga river valley amid hills to Damchara. The section between this station and Lumding was open for traffic on the 1st of December 1903. The railway first follows the right bank of the Jatinga, which runs between heavily-wooded hills, and the scenery begins to be very pretty.

All along the railway are posts showing the miles and quarter-miles from Chittagong, and the tunnels are also numbered; No. 2 being at the 272nd mile-post, and No. 3 goes through a landslip. Farther on, near another landslip, was the wreck of a recently derailed train. There was a hot controversy as to the cause of the accident, some ascribing it to excessive speed, others to faults in the permanent way. However that may be, the

Photographed by the Author.

BOATS AT CHANDPUR.

railway cuttings are certainly too steep, and work is going on all along this section reducing their pitch. The natives work with a sort of hoe called a khodali, and are usually armed with a big knife similar to the Burmese dha, which they call a dao. The valley broadens between the 278th post and Harangajao, which is between the 282nd and 283rd post, where the rail level is 489 feet above the sea.

There is plenty of big game to be found in Assam, including rhinoceros, elephant, leopards, the wild buffalo, and tigers. Shortly before we came through, a man had been found dead on the railway, mauled by a tiger, and we saw at Harangajao the body of a leopard which was killed on the line only a few hours before we arrived there. At this station two engines are attached to the train, one in front and one in back, and the real ascent begins. The gradient most of the way is 1 in 37, and there is a succession of tunnels and viaducts up to the summit, which is in tunnel No. 15, just before Jatinga station in the Cachar hills (294th mile), where the rail level is 1855 feet above the sea. The hills are less thickly wooded on the other side of the watershed, but there is more timber after Mahur. There are other streams to cross and further tunnels until, after threading No. 32, the line runs through a level jungle of bamboos and pampas-grass to Langting (343 miles). Three miles farther on there is a grave covered with a white marble cross by the side of the line.

After Lumding, where we changed into the dining-car, the railway goes across country to Dhansiri station, and then down the Dhansiri valley. After Manipur Road, from where there is a cart-road to Manipur going south-west to Kohima and then south, the railway runs in the Sibsagar district with the Naga hills lying to the east. It was about three o'clock in the morning when we pulled up at Kamarbandha Ali station, where we found kind friends whose tea-gardens are in this district.

Life in a bungalow on an Assam tea-garden is very much the same as it is in other remote districts in India. There are the same heavy risks to life and health taken lightly, and the same social trivialities taken seriously. There is the close clinging to the customs and habits of "home," together with a quickened ingenuity in adapting the local conditions to one's wants, or in adapting

Photographed by the Author.

ENTRANCE TO PLANTER'S BUNGALOW, ASSAM.

oneself to the local conditions. Of far deeper interest is the growth of the industry which has made possible these homes in the wilderness.

The romance of Assam is a romance of commerce, the history of a savage country brought under civilised rule through the cultivation, by alien labour, of a single product. It is true that Chittagong and part of the western districts of Assam were under a settled government long before tea was grown in the Brahmaputra valley, and it is true that oil and coal are found beneath the surface of the land upon which the Assamese grows for his own needs abundant crops of rice. But in spite of its other resources, the upper Brahmaputra would probably have been left in the undisturbed possession of the native tribes if it were not for the discovery of the native tea-plant, and the ultimate establishment of the tea-gardens. The tea-gardens are to Assam what the sugar-plantations are to the Hawaiian Islands, the source of its exports, its commercial prosperity, and its wealth.

In 1823 Mr. Robert Bruce heard that a tea-plant fifteen to twenty feet high, with a leaf nine inches long, was to be found growing wild in the jungles of Assam, and in 1824 his brother, Mr. C. A. Bruce, sent specimens to the government botanist at Calcutta. The botanist said the plant was a species of camellia, which was quite true, but he failed to recognise in it the tea camellia. Six years after Burma had ceded its Assamese territory an officer was sent to report on its possibilities, and Bruce again brought forward his camellia and insisted that it was tea. Two years later the government botanist admitted that Bruce's plant was the tea camellia, a committee was formed, and the first tea-garden was opened by the Indian Government in 1835 in Lakhimpur. One pound of tea made from the indigenous leaf was sent from this garden in the following year.

In 1840 the Assam Company was formed, and the Government turned over its experimental garden at Jaipur to the Company. The introduction of the Chinese tea-plant into India by Robert Fortune, another Scot, who imported 2000 tea-plants and 17,000 sprouting seeds into the North-West Provinces in 1851, and the employment of Chinese experience, and above all the experiments in the cultivation of hybrids, placed

Photographed by Mrs. J. W. H. McNab.

DOORIA TEA ESTATE, ASSAM—COOLIE WOMEN BRINGING IN TEA LEAF TO BE WEIGHED.

the cultivation upon a solid basis. The tea industry is also indebted to Sir Joseph Banks, to Colonel Kyd of the Calcutta Botanical Gardens, and to Dr. William Jameson of the Sararunpur Gardens for earlier experiments, as well as to Lord William Bentinck for official encouragement. In 1853 the weight of crop was about 300,000 pounds, in 1860 the tea grown in Assam and the rest of India had risen to about a million pounds, and in 1902 out of 525,000 acres of tea cultivated in the whole of India Assam accounted for about 340,000 acres; and out of a total production of less than 190 million pounds weight of leaf in that year, Assam grew over 132 million pounds.

While the seed trees in the nurseries grow to the height of 15 or 20 feet, the plant from which the leaf is plucked is seldom allowed to exceed 5 or 6 feet, and in the winter is pruned down to a couple of feet from the ground, or in extreme cases cut off close to the roots. In former times the bushes were grown as close together as 3 feet, in parallel lines crossing at right angles, so that four plants would form the corners of a 3-foot square: now they are planted 6 feet apart in diagonal lines, so that three plants occupy the angles of an equilateral triangle of 6 feet. Like the common English and Japanese camellias, the flower of the tea-plant has no scent.

All through the East, from India to Japan, tea is known as *cha* (or *chha*), the pronunciation of the Chinese ideograph in the Mandarin dialect, and the European name comes from the same ideograph, which is pronounced in the Amoy or Fuh-Kien dialect *te* (*tay*).

The tea industry in Assam has had to face many problems. The labour problem was one which early became a vital question, as the natives of Assam were quite content to cultivate the easily-grown rice and mustard which sufficed for their limited wants; and coolie labour, imported from Chhota Nagpur and other over-populated districts in India, became a necessity which caused many difficulties. We were told that 700,000 people imported from India are engaged in the Assam tea industry, and the total number employed in and around the gardens was, according to the census of 1901, 657,331, of whom 318,406, or nearly half, were females. Then the fixing of the rate of exchange between the rupee and the sovereign operated to increase the difficulties of competing with the Chinese growers, who get more silver money for a sovereign's worth of tea sold in London than can the Assam planters. Finally, there was the English tea-tax to be faced; and if any political economist remains in the belief that the consumer pays the import-tax, he had better stay away from Assam unless he is prepared to be converted from the error of his ways.

NOTE TO CHAPTER XII

DISTRICTS IN NEW PROVINCE OF EASTERN BENGAL AND ASSAM

Bakarganj.
Bogra.
Cachar.
Chittagong.
Chittagong Hill Tracts.
Dacca.
Darrang.
Dinajpur.
Faridpur.
Garo Hills.
Goalpara.
Jalpaiguri.
Kamrup.
Khasi and Jaintia Hills.
Lakhimpur.
Lushai Hills.
Maimansingh.
Maldah.
Naga Hills.
Noakhali.
Nowgong.
Pabna.
Rajshahi.
Rangpur.
Sibsagar.
Sylhet.
Tippera.

CHAPTER XIII

ASSAM—*continued*

Climate—The Brahmaputra from Nigri Ting to Dubri—A mournful river—Birds—The new province of Eastern Bengal and Assam.

THERE seems to be no question that the climate of the Brahmaputra Valley is very trying to Europeans in the rains; but in the cold weather, except for the morning fogs, nothing could be pleasanter. It may or may not be foggy in the early morning, but after chhota hazri, which in Assam means not the cup taken on rising but the big English breakfast, the sun is sure to come out and the temperature rise to between 60° and 70° in the shade, to fall again to 40° at night.

Not only is the temperature pleasant, but the air is bracing and surprisingly clear. And the clearness of this air is very deceptive. The snow-clad

Photographed by the Author.

A LANDING-PLACE ON THE BRAHMAPUTRA.

peaks of the Himalayas seen on a clear day N.N.E. from Nigri Ting ("Slave-girl Hill") are over a hundred miles away, but they appear to be only a quarter of that distance. The Brahmaputra is several miles broad after the rains, but in the cold weather one bank is frequently steep while the other consists of *chars* of pure sand left by the receding flood. The steep banks are over-grown with reeds and grasses, while the borders of the sand-banks are strewn with black chips guarded by a tiny wading-bird. The banks seem in the clear air to be about 10 feet high, and the reeds about 3 feet, when suddenly through an opening at the base of the reeds walks a full-grown man, and you find by the comparative height that the banks are 50 to 60 feet high and the reeds from 15 to 18 feet. Examined with your glasses the black chips turn into snub-nosed and sharp-nosed crocodiles (usually called alligators here), while the wader may be a bird as tall as a man.

As the Dutch reckoned the run of the canal-boats by the number of pipes smoked, so the Assamese are said to estimate distances by the number of "chews." This may account for the round numbers used in giving the distance from station to station on the river.

From Nigri Ting, where we embarked for our journey down the Brahmaputra, to Dhubri is about 325 miles, and we were made comfortable on the *Minhla*, the best boat of the Indian General Navigation and Railway Company's river fleet.

In spite of the great variety of bird life the Brahmaputra seems, as compared with the Irawadi, to be rather a mournful river. Wading birds, from the big herons, cranes, and storks to the little white herons and egrets—whose feathers, assumed only at the nesting season, make the fashionable "ospreys" or aigrettes—are seen everywhere. The brilliant Indian oriole or mango-bird and the maina, a member of the starling family, flash through the air, snake-birds cover the water, and the house-crows and jungle-crows haunt the landing-places; but for the first day hardly a boat is seen on the river, nor, except the temporary huts of the watermen, a single human habitation on the banks.

The landing-places have sometimes a moored flat alongside which the steamer makes fast, and at other places the steamer's nose is merely pushed

Photographed by the Author.

GAMIRIGHAT ON THE BRAHMAPUTRA.

into the bank and held there. The mournful character of the river is accentuated at the landings, where you witness pitiful scenes caused by the break-up of family ties when the coolies have finished their contract term and return home.

Below Nigri Ting the Dhansiri enters the Brahmaputra on the left bank, and the Lohit river, a continuation of the Subansiri, comes in on the opposite or north bank; but it is difficult to distinguish the tributaries from the re-entering branches of the river itself, which make many large islands on the way down. These branches sometimes change their course from year to year, but the Brahmaputra never in this respect rivals the Mississippi, whose main channel sometimes changes so as to transfer whole sections from one American state to another. All the forenoon the Himalayas are seen in the distant north, and in the afternoon the Naga Hills appear to the south.

At Bishnath, where we lay up for the night, we took on hundreds of cases of Pekoe, Broken Orange Pekoe, and Pekoe Souchong from the tea plantations. These extend on the north bank below Rangamati, and on the south bank to a point about 25 miles below Gauhati. At Sil Ghat the hills come down to the river, in which some rocks are seen for the first time. Tezpur, 75 miles below Nigri Ting, is built on a rocky bank, and from the steamer you can see permanent buildings and a railway. The second night we arrived at Gauhati, about 75 miles below Tezpur, Peacock Island and the wooded hills on both banks being dimly seen in the dusk. Tezpur has been identified with Sonitpur, "the city of blood," of the ancient legendary period.

Gauhati is a busy place, the terminus of the branch railway and the station for Shillong, the administrative headquarters of the Assam Government, situated 63 miles by road south in the Khasi Hills, on a plateau nearly 5000 feet above the sea. Here, on the 16th of October 1905, was published a Gazette extraordinary announcing the creation of the new province of Eastern Bengal and Assam under a Lieutenant-Governor and a Legislative Council. The new province, which was formed in spite of the organised opposition of the Bengali Babus, combines Assam's 56,000 square

Photographed by the Author.

VIEW ON THE BRAHMAPUTRA.

miles, containing a population of a little over six millions, with about 50,000 square miles containing over twenty-five million inhabitants taken from Bengal. The western border of the new province begins at the frontier of Bhutan, east of Darjiling, and runs south-west to Sahibganj on the Ganges. It then follows the course of the Ganges down to the deltaic branch called the Madhumati, which leaves the main stream above Goalundo, and the course of the latter which runs south to the Bay of Bengal. The proportion of Mohammedans to Hindus in the new province is as three to two, and the capital is fixed at the old Moslem town of Dacca in the delta of the Ganges and Brahmaputra.

The third morning we were caught in a fog, and had to anchor in the stream until about 10 o'clock. For another couple of hours a range of hills could be seen on the right bank, and detached hills on the left, while the river became more animated. We passed many boats, all of them being "tracked" or towed up against the stream. During the day we saw dolphins playing about in the river, and ghariyal or fish-eating crocodiles on the banks. In the afternoon the Garo Hills were in sight to the south, and the Bhutan Hills to the north, and at 4 o'clock we arrived at Dhubri. There we saw evidence of the great Bengal jute industry, and of the minor one of brickmaking. Having sent a request, in advance, to the station-master, we found attached to the train a through carriage for Silliguri, where we arrived early the next morning on the way to Darjiling. Ten weeks later, after having been as far north as the Khaibar Pass, we left Rawal Pindi for Kashmir.

NOTE TO CHAPTER XIII

TIME-TABLE OF BRAHMAPUTRA RIVER STEAMERS, WINTER, 1904-5

D.B. Dak Bungalow.
R.H. Rest House.
T.O. Telegraph Office.

Down River		Madras Time Leave
1st Day.	Dibrughur (Dibrugarh), D.B.	13
	Dehingmukh (Dihingmukh)	14.30
	Desangmukh (Disangmukh), R.H.	16.30
	Dekumukh (Dikhumukh)	17.30
	Jhansimukh (Janjimukh)	18.30
	Kolomabari (Kamlabari)	19.30
2nd Day.	Kokeelamukh (Kokilamukh), D.B.	6
	Nigriting (Nigri Ting), R.H.	8
	Dhansirimukh, R.H.	11
	Gamirighat (Gomiri Ghat)	13
	Behalimukh, R.H.	14
	Bishnath (Biswanath), T.O.	16

Down River		Madras Time Leave
3rd Day.	Silghat, D.B.	8
	Tezpur, D.B.	10
	Singrighat (Singari Ghat)	12.30
	Rangamatighat, R.H.	16
	Gauhati	18
	Sualkuchi (Saulkusi)	21
	Polashbari (Palasbari), T.O.	21.20
	Kholabandha	0.30
4th Day.	Dalgoma	2
	Goalpara, T.O.	3.15
	Bilashipari (Bilasipara)	5.15
	Dhubri Ghat, D.B.	9
5th Day.	Jagannathgunge, T.O.	5
	Serajgunge (Sirajganj), D.B.	6
	Goalundo, T.O.	11

Up River		Leave
1st Day.	Goalundo	5.30
2nd „	Dhubri Ghat	9.30
3rd „	Polashbari	4.10
4th „	Tezpur	9
5th „	Dhansirimukh	7
6th „	Desangmukh	5.10
		Arrive
„ „	Dibrughur	19

CHAPTER XIV

THE ROAD TO KASHMIR

The Happy Valley—The city of Sri—Dhanjibhoy and Son—A tramp in the snow—Murree—Kohala Bridge

THERE are three Kashmirs—the state, the valley, and the city. The state of Kashmir had a population in 1901 of over 1,157,000, of whom all but 150,000 speak Kashur, as the Kashmiri language is called, while the territories of the Maharaja of Jammu and Kashmir, including Malakand, Chitral, and adjoining districts, cover an area of 80,900 square miles, and contain 2,906,000 inhabitants, of whom over ninety per cent are Mohammedans, nearly all of the Sunni sect.

"The Happy Valley of Kashmir" lies at a mean elevation of about 6000 feet above the sea, the lowest point being about 5200 feet. The floor of the valley is about 85 miles long and

22 miles wide; but from peak to peak of the surrounding mountains, which rise thousands of feet on all sides, the valley measures about 120 miles from south-east to north-west, is 75 miles wide in its broadest part, and has an area of 4500 square miles. In speaking of Kashmir, it is this valley which is usually meant.

In the middle of the length of the valley near its eastern border of mountains, at an elevation of 5276 feet above the sea, is Srinagar, founded by King Pravarasena II. in the sixth century, and at first named after him Pravarapura. The present name means "The City of Sri" (Lakshmi), the Goddess of Wealth and Beauty, although commonly supposed to be derived from Surjyanagar, which would be translated "The City of the Sun."

Although sometimes called Kashmir City, it is generally known as Srinagar, and the name as pronounced by the natives falls upon the stranger's ear as "Seroon-nug-ger." The city has been the capital since its foundation, and it is to-day the summer capital of H.H. the Maharaja, Jammu being his winter capital. In 1901 the population of Srinagar was 122,000.

The road into Kashmir by the Jehlam river is Messrs. Dhanjibhoy and Son, the Imperial Carrying Company, Limited, writ large. Dhanjibhoy, the mail agent and proprietor of the tonga service, has the manners of a diplomat, the powers of an autocrat, and the inherited shrewdness of the Parsi. "Son" is still in leading-strings. At first we were told that we must give up the road by way of Murree owing to the heavy snowfall, and make special arrangements for conveyances by way of Hasan Abdal and Abbottabad. The time-table by the latter route would have been—first day, 42 miles from Hasan Abdal to Abbottabad; second day, 16 miles to Mansira; third day, 18 miles to Garhi Habibulla; fourth day, 22 miles, or 98 miles in all, to Domel, where the road joins the one from Murree; and three more days to do the 110 miles to Srinagar.

Dhanjibhoy flattered our vanity by observing that three such fine young men would probably not mind the hardships of the Murree route to Srinagar, which he, on second thoughts, was of the opinion we might reach in four days. The usual time is sixty hours, including stoppages for

Photographed by the Author.

OUR TONGA WITH LUGGAGE TIED OUTSIDE.

meals, that is, six hours from Rawal Pindi to Murree, two days from Murree to Baramula, and six hours more to Srinagar. The mail tongas which travel all day and night can go through in half the time. In the end we decided to take our chances by the Murree route, and left the hotel at Rawal Pindi at half-past three in the afternoon of the 25th of February.

Our servants had refused to go with us, as they were afraid of the cold and of the dangers of the road, so we three started off with our luggage in a special tonga. A special tonga for three from Rawal Pindi costs 130 rupees, or just two-thirds of a rupee per mile for the 195 miles. For such parts of the road as were impracticable for tongas, we were to be refunded a proportionate amount. Once on board the tonga we were free to start as early as we liked, stop for the night at any dak bungalow on the road, drive on as long as the light lasted, and halt for meals where we pleased.

Dhanjibhoy was careful to point out that all he agreed to do was to supply the vehicle, give us relays of quiet, well-broken-in ponies, and a competent driver. He "did not insure our lives," and we must take all risks. It is only fair to say that he carried out his part of the contract as well as could be expected. It is true that one of his tongas broke down, that the drivers were of unequal ability, that most of the ponies were jibbers, and one pair of them proved unmanageable and detained us in the road for a couple of hours; but such experiences are common to all travellers by road.

In order to visit Kashmir it is provided that a pass shall be procured from the Assistant Resident in Kashmir, who lives in Srinagar, and when applying by letter for such a pass you are required to state your rank or profession and the object of your visit (sport, health, pleasure, or business). The real object of the pass is to bring you under the control of the Resident, by obtaining your agreement to observe the conditions and rules, which have not otherwise the force of laws, considered necessary for the preservation of game, the maintenance of order, and the fostering of good relations with the natives. Owing to delay of mails on the road our passes had not arrived before we started, so we left without having any, and when we reported ourselves at Srinagar were informed it would hardly be necessary for us to have a pass for the short period of our stay.

Murree lies to the north-east of Rawal Pindi, and is about 7300 feet above the sea. The distance is usually given as 37 miles, but Murree extends over nearly 6 miles from the brewery to the south end of the Kuldanna cantonment, so that the distance is sometimes given at 35, and sometimes at 40 miles. Every 5 or 6 miles there is a relay of horses, and the change is made in from two to six minutes; anything over three minutes being considered slow. A relay is called a *dak*, and the word is commonly used in India to denote the distance between relays or the length of a journey. The first dak out of Rawal Pindi is just over 6 miles, and the road seems to go slightly downhill. Half-way between the first and second daks the road is fairly level, and at a bridge across the stream we saw a large caravan of camels. After the second dak there is a short ascent over a range of hills, and a descent of about a mile to the bridge at the stone marking the distance from Rawal Pindi as 13·3, or 13 miles and 3 furlongs.

From this bridge to the third dak at the 17th milestone, where toll has to be paid, the road is mostly uphill, with views to the right over the hills; but 6 furlongs beyond this dak the road descends to a stream, and then comes 2 miles ascent and a mile downhill to the bridge over the stream at 20·4.

The bridges crossed from time to time are over the tributaries and main stream of the Karung river, whose valley the road follows up to Tret. Ascending through tree-covered slopes for about a mile, we arrived at the fourth dak; and at the 22nd milestone, where the road is high above the river, there are views behind us over the distant hills, and below us of the road by which we had come. Then we descend to another bridge and go up the left bank of the stream, ascending zigzags at the 24th milepost, and arriving at the Thet dak bungalow at twenty minutes past six. The actual time from the hotel was two hours and fifty minutes, and the distance nearly 26 miles, so that the rate was about 9 miles an hour, including stops, and we had reached an elevation of nearly 4000 feet above the sea. There was

Photographed by the Author.

COOLIES CARRYING OUR LUGGAGE OVER THE SNOW.

some snow to be seen on the saddle of the hill in front of the dak bungalow at Tret, but the sun had been uncomfortably hot during the day, and there was no sign of snow on the road.

The next morning we left Tret at half-past seven, and got to Gohragully in little over an hour. From milestones 27 to 29, where the road zigzags up, there are fine views over the plains to Rawal Pindi, south of south-west, and to the isolated mountains west of south-west. Above milestone 30 there was snow and ice on the road, and two miles beyond the tonga stopped close by the round, stone watch-tower, at Gohragully, built at time of the Mutiny, about a mile below Murree brewery. There we engaged coolies to carry our luggage, and riding ponies for ourselves.

The established charge for riding ponies with "European saddles" is one rupee per stage; for baggage ponies or mules, eight annas; and for coolies carrying twenty-five sirs, say fifty pounds weight, of luggage, four annas. An extra payment of an anna to a good coolie is considered a satisfactory tip. The tonga drivers look for a tip, but the ostlers or syces expect nothing. Owing to the bad state of the road we promised our coolies double pay if they made good time. We paid two rupees each for the hire of the ponies to Bagla, and had already mounted when the owner refused to let us start, unless we each paid another rupee. As we knew it would not do to go faster than our luggage, and as the ponies were poor brutes, we concluded not to insist on our right to them, but demanded our money back and started off on foot about nine o'clock. It was just so much saved, as the road above the brewery was quite impracticable for ponies, and we must have abandoned them. The snow on the road had a narrow track through it which had been trodden by the coolies, who carried the mail-bags, walking in single file. These footsteps were two or three feet above the surface of the road, and if we placed one foot before the other carefully we found a solid, if slippery, foothold, but any deviation landed us in the soft, deep snow. The ponies would simply have floundered about, so we were better off without them.

The mountains on our side of the valley are

here covered with trees, but those across the valley to the north-west are bare. We reached milestone 34 at ten o'clock, and about a quarter of an hour later passed round a shoulder of the mountain at Basur Gali, and turned to the right out of the tonga road, then up through the trees to Trinity Church, Murree, which we reached at twenty minutes past eleven, the snow becoming deeper as we proceeded. We retraced our steps from the church to Chamber's Hotel, where we found some food, and passed the church again on our way to Bagla. It took us nearly an hour to get to milestone 39 at the cross-roads on the ridge, and half an hour later we took a path to the right through the woods, and down by a short cut with some breakneck bits at the finish, where the next traveller was lowered with a rope from tree to tree, to the tonga road close to milestone 43 which we reached at half-past two. Half an hour later we found a tonga at Bagla between milestones 44 and 45, and after changing our wet shoes and putting on some warm wraps we started on the way down to Kohala. We had had a hot sun all day up to this time, and we suffered more from the heat than the cold in plodding through the snow; but now it became overclouded, and we had at first some difficulty in keeping warm. Four miles lower down, after the first dak, the road was clear of snow, and at milestone 51 the Jehlam could be seen thousands of feet below.

The general direction of the road from Murree to Kohala is north-north-east, descending the flank of the mountains on the west or right bank of the Jehlam, which flows, a little to the east of south, between Domel and the town of Jehlam on the North-Western Railway, and forms the western boundary of Kashmir. Across the valley to the eastward we could see the peaks of the Pir Panjal range of mountains in the Punch district of Kashmir. Through these mountains is the old Imperial Road, starting from Gujrat and running about 160 miles to Srinagar, by which the Moguls visited Kashmir from the Punjab.

From Murree the road runs downhill all the way to Kohala, which is about 2000 feet above the level of the sea, with nearly level stretches between milestones 54 and 55, and also between the small bridge at milestone 63 and Kohala Bridge. The

Photographed by the Author.

"SOLOMON'S THRONE"—SRINAGAR MERCHANTS IN FOREGROUND.

culverts and bridges are of stone, and the road is kept in very good condition. At the sides were heaps of road-metal ready to be spread over the surface before the rush of visitors annually expected in the latter half of March. At milestone 52 the flank of the mountain above us was free from snow, and we passed through a grove of trees. There is a dak at 55·7, and a beautiful view down to the river with the vivid green of young paddy-fields in the valley, and snow on the mountains in the distant background. A couple of miles farther on the road itself forms the bed of a small stream, which is conducted over on a surface of large stones; at milestone 63·4 Kohala Bridge comes in sight, and a short distance from it down the stream are the remains of the piers of the old bridge built in 1871. Before arriving at the bridge there was a bad subsidence on the river side of the road where the embankment had given way.

Kohala is a quaint little village plastered against the hillside, the houses rising one above the other, and the goats were feeding on the flat, mud roofs, characteristic of the Jehlam valley. The dak bungalow is on the hillside above the road, as is also the post office. Srinagar lies over the mountains almost due east from Kohala, but the road first runs north up the Jehlam Valley for over twenty miles before finding a break in the mountain barrier.

CHAPTER XV

KOHALA BRIDGE TO CHAKOTI

The Jehlam and Kishanganga—A dangerous road—Domel—The great gorge—An accident to the tonga driver—Chakoti.

THE iron bridge across the Jehlam at Kohala, built in 1895, toll one rupee, is 64 miles 348 feet from Rawal Pindi, and in calculating the distances from point to point, these odd feet and the length of the bridge are disregarded. On the Kashmir side a new series of milestones from the bridge to Baramula begins, and between these milestones the road is divided into sections of about 100 feet numbered 1 to 52. The road up the left bank of the Jehlam from Kohala to Baramula, which took ten years to build and cost about £185,000, was opened in 1889, but cart traffic only began in September 1890, and before the latter date no wheeled vehicles had ever run into or out of Kashmir. Nor, in fact, were there any roads for wheeled traffic in Kashmir itself. The waterways formed the principal means of transportation within the valley, and goods imported and exported were carried on men's backs. There was an old road, available for coolie traffic, down the right bank of the Jehlam from Baramula. Beyond Kohala the road runs north at first, and is cut for the most part in the face of the cliffs, sometimes high above the river and sometimes approaching its level.

The scenery after crossing the bridge is very fine, the turbulent river rushing through its narrow bed below, the hills rising steeply from it on either side, and in the distant background across the river to the north-west are higher snow-capped mountains. After the 1st milestone is the Maharaja's rest-house at Barasalla, and near it the road was nearly blocked by two great rocks that had fallen from the cliffs above. Then the road crosses a bridge and threads a tunnel, and after passing other rock-falls we arrived at the 3rd milestone, where a bad landslip above and below the road left barely room for the tonga to pass in

Photographed by the Author.

THE MUSEUM AND SOLOMON'S THRONE FROM THE RIVER.

the narrow space between the fallen rocks and the crumbling edge of the road. Just before the 5th milestone is another tunnel, and then a good stretch of road for two or three miles when we crossed a small plateau, passing through a grove of trees, and drove by the village of Chattar down a zigzag road, on which is the 8th milestone, to a couple of bridges over a tributary stream. The 9th milestone is between these bridges, and there was a fall of rocks on the road before reaching the 10th milestone, and several falls between the 10th and 11th. Less than a mile beyond the latter is Dulai, where we stopped for the night at the very nice dak bungalow prettily situated on the river-bank, and after a fairly good dinner we turned in, satisfied with having done a good day's work.

It began to rain during the night, the wind rising to half a gale, and when we left at eight o'clock the next morning it was still raining. There was a bridge to cross before the 12th milestone and at the 14th milestone there were bad falls of rocks on the road. A mile and a half farther on is the village of Rara, near which a stream enters the Jehlam on the opposite bank. The road then ascends high above the river and is cut in the face of the cliffs. Between milestones 16 and 17 were more rock-falls, and after the latter came a dak, then a long tunnel followed by a shorter tunnel at milestone 18, and more rock-falls before and after the next milestone. After milestone 20 the road runs through a short cutting and enters the more open valley at the junction of the Jehlam and Kishanganga rivers. The latter comes down from the north; and the former from the east or rather south-east, so that its left bank here forms an acute angle. Milestone 21 is at the bridge, across the Jehlam, by which the road from the north through Garhi Habibulla and by the left bank of the Kishanganga joins the Murree road. The Domel dak bungalow is near the bridge, and farther along the Kashmir road is a toll-gate and custom-house, where we had to pay three rupees toll. The distant mountains up both river valleys were capped with snow, and from all we could hear, the road was no better by way of Abbottadad than by the way we had come.

The Jehlam, which is also known as the Behat,

or by its Sanskrit name Vitasta, has a local name between Domel and Baramula, where it is called Kashur Darya. From Domel to Uri the road runs south-east, and for the first six miles to Tindali the mountains alternately recede from and approach the river, forming small valleys. The high mountain tops north of milestone 24 were covered with snow, and in the river opposite the next milestone is an island which is submerged when the river is in flood, and there is a similar island opposite the next dak, at 28½ miles. There was a rock-fall near Tindali, after which we passed lines of new trees planted along the roadside, and then two bad falls of rock on the road, one before and one after the 30th milestone. Three miles farther on the road gets down nearly to the level of the river, and at milestone 34 is Garhi. Garhi means a small fort and is frequently used in Kashmiri names of places. Here we were delayed twenty minutes, while the tonga wheels were greased and a new driver taken on, and we had a chance to walk to the suspension bridge for foot-passengers across the Jehlam, and enjoy the view down-stream closed by the distant snow-covered mountain tops. It had stopped raining by the time we left Domel, but came down again before we left Garhi.

Half a mile beyond Garhi the road ascends a detached hill by zigzags, and goes through the shoulder of it by an open cutting on to one of the small plateaus or river terraces called by the natives karewas or udars. These are seen sometimes on one side of the river and sometimes on both sides up to Baramula, and appear to be the old bed of the river, high up above the present stream which flows in the deep gorge below. There is a grove of trees on this plateau before milestone 36, and at 38 miles the road serves as the bed of a small stream which crosses it. The road zigzags down before the next milestone and up again after it, and there is another grove of trees before the dak at Saran, 39¼ miles. Beyond the 40th milestone the road turns sharply to the right and is cut in the sheer face of the cliffs, which form a side gorge entering the main defile at right angles; and at milestone 42 there is a magnificent view looking backward down the Jehlam. In fact the scenery is exceptionally wild

Photographed by the Author.

THE MUSEUM, SRINAGAR.

and grand throughout the whole of this dak to Hattian, 45 miles. Just before Hattian is an iron girder bridge, and above Hattian, but on the other side of the Jehlam, is a fine waterfall in a cleft of the mountains.

After Zeli, 47 miles, are the recently finished towers of a new suspension bridge across the Jehlam, and opposite milestone 48 a tributary torrent enters the other bank. Then came a very bad mile. A big rock had fallen on the road and blocked half of it, while farther on the road itself had partly fallen into the river. At the 50th milestone is the highest waterfall on the route, coming into the river close to the road, and at the next milestone is another waterfall. Just before the latter is the dak at Chinari, and there our driver, the best whip and finest post-horn performer we found on the road, came to grief. He was holding up the tonga pole during the change of horses, and one was about to be secured when the brute plunged and broke away, allowing the heavy pole to fall to the ground, and as it fell, one of the driver's fingers was caught between the metal bands by which the cross-piece or yoke is fastened to the pole, and the fleshy top of it including the nail torn completely off. He stood dazed for an instant, looking at the protuding bone —it was the middle finger of the left hand—then calmly stooped down and fished out the torn flesh from between the metals, and stuck it back again. After washing the finger we dressed it in lint and salve, tied it up with adhesive tape, and wrapped it in a handkerchief. There was no other driver to be had and the nearest doctor was at Uri, so with this rough dressing he started to drive us eighteen miles over a dangerous road, strewn with fallen rocks and broken away in places, in a storm of rain which turned to heavy wet snow during the afternoon.

There was a big rock on the road in the first mile out of Chinari, and four cascades close to the road in the mile following. Up to milestone 54, where there were fresh falls of rock, the condition of the road was very bad, and then came another cascade followed by an inprovement in the road to Chakoti, $55\frac{3}{4}$ miles, where we had tiffin at the dak bungalow prettily situated where a mountain stream enters the river.

CHAPTER XVI

CHAKOTI TO SRINAGAR

The Jehlam gorge—A breakdown—Uri—Oriental cunning—Avalanches and landslides—Rampur—The Temple of Buniar—Baramula—Patan—Srinagar.

THE rain had changed to snow by the time we finished tiffin at Chakoti, and it continued snowing all the evening. But in spite of all difficulties our wounded driver cheerily sounded his horn and drove us out of Chakoti, over the bridge by the waterfall, and along the treacherous road which runs for miles under the conglomerate cliffs. After crossing the old wooden bridge near Uppi, 57½ miles, the cliffs above the road increase in height, the road got rapidly worse, and just before milestone 59 there was another bad cave in the road. The next five miles were dangerous to a degree, and it is a wonder that we got through with whole skins.

The road gets nearer to the river level at the 60th milestone, where there are grand cliffs on the opposite side of the river which here runs, nearly straight, through a magnificent gorge extremely wild and impressive. After crossing a bridge and changing horses, we began what proved to be the worst dak. At milestone 61 the road was very bad, and the next mile, all under the crumbling cliffs after passing Dardkob and another bridge, was the most dangerous mile of the day. At milestone 62 a boulder, half a ton in weight, lay in the middle of the road, and we bumped on for another two miles over smaller fallen rocks, which somewhat distracted our attention from the grand views down the straight reach of river flowing at the bottom of the gorge far below.

The biggest fallen rock, bigger than the tonga itself, lay in the road between the milestones 64 and 65. At the end of another mile we seemed to have got over the difficult part, and our driver had just whipped his horses up, for a dash to the last dak before Uri, when off flew the tire of the near wheel, and before the driver could pull up the wheel had been broken to pieces, and we came to

Photographed by the Author.

VIEW FROM THE BUND, SRINAGAR.

a standstill. There was no other damage done, and our resourceful driver sent the syce—the groom who travels from dak to dak with each pair of horses and hangs on to the tonga as best he can—on with the horses to the dak, which was fortunately near at hand. But there was no tonga to be had there, and an hour passed before we were on our way again in a covered bullock-cart with our wet luggage, most of which had been exposed all day, on the outside of the tonga, to the rain and snow.

After the next dak the road runs over the plateau upon which the village of Islamabad is situated, on a causeway built across paddy-fields; then comes the bridge where the Jehlam makes a right-angled turn at milestone 68; and after the next milestone is the Uri dak bungalow, where we put up for the night. Sending the driver off to the doctor with a good round tip for his plucky behaviour, we unpacked our luggage and spread the wet things out to dry. Fortunately, some of our packages were water-tight, or we should have had a bad night of it.

Uri occupies a commanding position at the junction of the Jehlam and Haji Pir valleys. The road, which runs south-east from Domel to Uri, changes its general direction to north-east between Uri and Baramula. The Haji Pir river flows into the Jehlam from the south, coming down from the pass of the same name.

The next morning we had an experience of Oriental cunning. We had asked the tahsildar the night before to provide us with coolies to carry our luggage as the road was blocked for wheeled traffic between Uri and Baramula, and we knew we should have close on thirty miles to walk through the snow. We had some hopes of doing it in one day, if we could make an early start; but when the coolies arrived in the morning, the native in charge of the dak bungalow shepherded them into an out-house, and kept us kicking our heels until after ten o'clock waiting for the coolies to turn up. Finally, suspecting the trick, we offered him a reward if he procured us the number of coolies we wanted within five minutes, and, sure enough, out they came from their hiding-place and picked up their loads. We paid the promised reward, but on our return journey gave him good advice instead of a tip, so that in the end he gained nothing.

From the Uri dak bungalow, which we left at a quarter-past ten, we took a short cut down to the Haji Pir river, crossing it on the coolies' shoulders and nearly getting a ducking, and then up again to the road, which we found in a very bad condition. Not only were we obliged to walk in a narrow track through snow and slush continually up to our ankles and sometimes up to our knees, but the road was blocked in many places by avalanches and landslides, and in other places had caved in and fallen away. And the cliffs above us were still crumbling as we walked along, so that in many places we had to watch our opportunity and run past the falling earth and snow. As it turned out, we had no really narrow escapes, although there were many fresh falls of rock on the road since yesterday's snow, and from milestone 76, which we reached at half-past twelve, we could see on the precipitous flank of the mountain ahead the fresh path of an enormous avalanche. Landslips again occurred near here in September 1905. The best pace we could get out of our coolies was two miles an hour, and when one of us forged ahead to get some food prepared at Rampur, three miles in an hour was the utmost that could be done. Just after milestone 76 are the ruins of a square stone temple with an arched entrance the top of which is formed by a single large stone. The mountains on our side of the valley are more heavily clothed with trees, and after passing Uri deodars are seen on the hills above, but on all sides they were covered with snow from their summits to the river's edge.

From milestone 79 the road was less dangerous, although the snow was much deeper. In places there was at least six feet of it in the drifts on the road, and at one place, between milestones 81 and 82, where an avalanche had formed an inclined plane from the cliffs above the road to the river below, the snow was fully twenty feet deep where we had to climb over it. Just beyond the 80th milestone is the hamlet of Uruboha, and between it and Rampur there are grand rock cliffs standing back from the road and rising up in sheer precipices. It was a quarter to four by the time the last coolie reached Rampur, so we had to be satisfied with a short day's work, and resigned ourselves to the comforts of dry foot-gear before a roaring wood-fire

Photographed by the Author.

SRINAGAR BUND FROM THE MUSEUM.

in the old dak bungalow, with a hearty meal to follow and a good night's rest.

March came in "like a lamb," and at nine o'clock on the morning of the first of the month we started to walk from Rampur to Baramula, fifteen and a half miles by the road. But we took a short cut just after leaving the dak bungalow, turning to the left out of the road and going down a ravine to a small bridge and up again, by a narrow path through a jumble of big rocks, to the road at milestone 85 near the Temple of Buniar built, according to tradition, by the Pandava brethren. The temple as it stands to-day is a central shrine in the middle of a square courtyard surrounded by cells. The central shrine, which is square and has no spire, is built on a plinth, and the interior, which contains a linga, is approached by a flight of steps. The temple and cells are built of blue limestone. In the enclosure behind the shrine are thirteen cells ; on each side are fifteen, and the entrance to the courtyard in front of the central shrine is flanked by five cells on either hand, making fifty-three in all ; and, as far as we could see, the cells were all empty. The doorways are finished with a trefoil arch, formed by large stones laid in horizontal courses, and embellished with a pyramidal hood-moulding or pediment. Such doorways and fluted columns, with wide intervals between them, form the characteristic features of the ancient stone architecture of Kashmir.

Beyond Buniar the valley opens, then comes the village of Nowshera, and two miles farther on ($88\frac{3}{4}$) the village of Chantamula. Then "the March lamb" began to shed its fleece, and at noon it was snowing hard. Between milestones 91 and 92 the valley opens out on our side, while across the river is a wide plateau which ends in cliffs opposite Hichama (92 miles), where our side becomes still more open. We found at Hichama the mail tonga, which had forced its way down through the snow from Baramula, and also a sahib who was going towards Rampur on a pony.

The road has a heavy gradient after Hichama, and the valley closes in again near Sheri but afterwards opens out, and the road was fairly easy up to the cross-road to Baramula Bridge. We reached Dhanjibhoy's office at a quarter-past three; but it was nearly half-past four before we had had some tea, changed our clothes, settled with our coolies, and left Baramula for the drive of thirty-four miles south-east to the hotel at Srinagar. Meanwhile it had stopped snowing, but there was snow on the road up to the milestone which marks the distance from Kohala as 100 miles, and from Sher Garhi, Srinagar, as 31 miles. After that the road was free from snow, although the ground was covered on both sides.

All the way along, with few breaks, the nearly straight road, nine miles of which was under water during the flood of September 1905, is lined with a row of poplars on each side. Wild ducks, jackals, and large wading-birds were seen from time to time between the dirty villages; but by the time we had left the hills and passed through Sangrama it began to snow again, and we could not see far from the road. We were still a long way from Srinagar when night fell; the dak bungalow and the ruins of the temples at Patan, built over a thousand years ago by Samkara-varman and his queen, Sugandha, were indistinctly seen, and by the time we reached Haritrat it was quite dark. We arrived at Mirgund, the last dak, at a quarter-past eight, and there the horses were changed by the light of straw and pinewood torches, but we got a good pair at last, and arrived at Nedou's Hotel, Srinagar, within an hour. Having telegraphed from Baramula that we were coming on, we found refreshments and beds awaiting us, and did justice to both.

We were informed that the mails which left Rawal Pindi on Sunday, February 26, arrived at Srinagar in the first hour of Thursday morning, taking over seventy-four hours to come through instead of the usual thirty, or at most thirty-six, hours.

NOTE TO CHAPTER XVI

Stages on Kashmir Road

Distances from Rawal Pindi.		Above sea. 1726	From Kohala Bridge.
25½	Tret	3400	
31¾	Gohragully (Ghora Gully)		
37	Murree (Mari)	7300	
44½	Bagla		
64	Kohala	2000	
65½	Barasala (Barsala)	...	1½
71¾	Chattar	...	7¾
73¼	Kullian	...	9¼
75¾	Dulai	2180	11¾
79½	Rara	...	15½
85¼	Domel	2320	21¼

Photographed by the Author.

SHER GARHI PALACE, SRINAGAR.

Distances from Rawal Pindi.		Above sea.	From Kohala Bridge.
91¼	Tindali (Tinali)	...	27¼
98	Garhi (Gurhi)	2750	34
103¼	Saran	...	39¼
109	Hattian (Hatian)	...	45
111	Zeli (Neli)	3080	47
115	Chinari	...	51
119¾	Chakoti (Chakuti)	3780	55¾
121½	Uppi (Opi)	...	57½
125¼	Dardkob	...	61¼
130½	Islamabad	...	66½
133	Uri (Urie)	4425	69
144	Uruboha (Urambu)	...	80
146¼	Rampur	4825	82¼
147¾	Buniar (Bhaniar)	...	83¾
150¾	Nowshera (Naoshera)	...	86¾
152¾	Chantamula (Ghaut Malla)	...	88¾
156	Hichama (Kechama)	...	92
158¾	Sheri (Shir)	...	94¾
161¾	Baramula	5150	97¾
168	Sangrama	...	104
173	Bulgaon	...	109
175¾	Palhalan	...	111¾
177¾	Patan	5300	113¾
183¼	Haritrat (Harprat)	...	119¼
187¼	Mirgund (Merigond)	...	123¼
195	Srinagar, Sher Garhi	5235 to	131
196	Srinagar Hotel	5276	132

CHAPTER XVII

THE VENICE OF THE EAST

Early birds—Merchants and tourists—Thieves and swindlers —Curios and trophies—Punts and house-boats.

THE sun rose in a cloudless sky the following morning. The news of our arrival had spread in the curious rapid way such things get about in the East, and every merchant in Srinagar knew that the first guests of the season had made an appearance at the hotel. Other visitors were already on the way, but we were the first tourists.

The first sportsman to arrive at the hotel for the summer shooting season of 1905 was a German officer, a lieutenant in the Uhlans, who left Rawal Pindi, Saturday morning, February 25, and arrived by way of Abbottabad at Srinagar, Friday night, March 3. The next day two American gentlemen turned up. The shooting licence for the summer season covers the eight months from March 15 to November 15. The first comer has the choice of ground, and when he has selected his nullah and paid sixty rupees for his licence, he may kill as many as six each of the goral, thar, ibex, and burhel, four red bear, two heads each of sharpu, markhor, and barasingh, but only one serow and one Ovis Ammon.

In the early morning the merchants invaded the hotel, swarmed in the passages, and besieged us in our rooms. Every face showed a pair of hawk's eyes, keen and alert; but there was a gleam of cheerful exultation which seemed to say "Now is the winter of our discontent made glorious summer." When we left the hotel they followed us to the boat, and when we started down the canal to the river they pursued us in other boats. Relays watched for us from lofty windows above the river and joined in the chase, dodging through the narrow streets behind the houses facing the river and reappearing at each landing-place, while one enterprising dealer pursued us along the bank mounted on a horse. At last we landed at the Zaina Kadal and were brought to bay. A score of dirty hands thrust greasy cards in our faces, double that number of voices invited us to visit as many shops, each "the best in Kashmir," and those who stood nearest whispered in our ear that the rest were all thieves and swindlers.

That the Kashmiris are persistent, voluble, and quick-witted is easy to discover; that they are a dirty, cringing, spiritless lot is easy to see; and that they are untruthful and dishonest is easy to believe. If the Kashmiri merchants enjoy the reputation of being the most unconscionable rogues, it is mainly their own fault, and every merchant in Srinagar is ready to admit that, with one exception, they are all even worse than reputed.

As a matter of fact, the Kashmiris do carry their swindling a point beyond our experience of any other land, for in all our travels we never found another country where the post office is used for the issue of false coin. At the Baramula post office on the way up two bad rupees were given in the change for a sovereign, and at Srinagar one bad rupee. The one received at the latter place is kept as a souvenir, the two received at

Photographed by the Author.

FATTEH KADAL, ONE OF THE BRIDGES AT SRINAGAR.

Baramula were afterwards taken back and good ones given us in exchange.

We visited many shops in Srinagar, going through filthy alleys, courtyards, and passages, always followed by the merchants of the city, and it would almost appear that the only firm unrepresented in the crowd was the one whose notice, posted in the hotel, read as follows:—"For the convenience of the European residents and visitors I am requesting that I will left Srinagar valley on the 15th instant for Sialkot."

We were fortunate enough to meet at the hotel a sportsman who had been driven in by stress of weather from his camp in the nullah, where he had been "sleeping with the game" during the winter, and who gave us the advantage of his experience. Under his guidance we saw the sights of Srinagar, and were enabled to make a few purchases of native work at reasonable prices; and when we left in a house-boat for Baramula he came part of the way with us.

In the metal-work shops we saw samovars of Russian pattern, and a "fire-devil" in the shape of a metal bird filled with water and placed on a charcoal fire, which it automatically blows in a similar manner to a pair of bellows.

We purchased finely-chased silver on the basis of twelve annas per tola, embroideries on our estimate of the number of days' work at four annas a day, as well as enamels, lacquer work (*nakash*), papier-maché (*kar-i-kalamdani*), and carved wood at moderate prices. We also bought some skins, including one of a fine snow leopard (safed chetah or ramahun) from Ladakh, of Mohammed Baba, the taxidermist, at whose shop we saw a fairly complete collection of the larger mammalia of Kashmir. Among others were the markhor, whose broad spiral horns form a wide V; the barasingh, or Kashmir stag; the Ovis Ammon (or nyan), a wild sheep with enormous horns curving down until the points face towards the front; the burhel (or narpu), whose horns curve boldly outward; and the other variety of wild sheep called the sharpu (or urin), whose horns curve back in a semi-circle. There were also heads of the Tibetan antelope or goa, whose ringed horns go straight up making a tall V with the tops curved towards each other, and the ibex (kale mayar) from Baltistan whose broad horns curve backwards like those of the sharpu. Specimens of the goral, serow, chakor, manaul, musk deer or kusturah, thar, wolf, fox, bear, and loh or Kashmiri fox could also be inspected.

Srinagar is indeed a filthy town, and it is no wonder that it is considered unhealthy, or that thousands perish of cholera and small-pox. But we saw it at a very bad time, when the heavy fall of snow was melting and had been trodden into slush. Even so, it is not as bad as some Chinese cities, while the river running through it enables one to avoid long walks in the streets and gives it a Venetian picturesqueness. The curious tumble-down wooden buildings propped up with long timbers, the balconies projecting from unexpected places, the peculiar bridges or kadals (pronounced "cuddles"), the stone landing-places and steps, the floating latrines, and the shikaras and dungas all combine to form a picture of exceptional quaintness.

In this veritable "Venice of the East" the place of the gondola is taken by the shikara, which is nothing more or less than a Thames punt, propelled by paddles (*kur*). These paddles have heart-shaped blades fashioned in the form of the leaf of the water-lily and fastened to the handle with a band. The coolies sit on their haunches fore and aft and use three different strokes—the plain backward dig followed by a clean lift from the water; the dig and lift followed by feathering in a semi-circle; and the dig and lift followed by a peculiar twiddle. The manjhi or boatman is paid a small sum for the use of his boat, and you employ as many coolies as you want for paddling at four annas a day—the usual wage of an able-bodied Kashmiri.

Photographed by the Author.

MOSQUE OF SHAH HAMADAN, SRINAGAR.

CHAPTER XVIII

THE BRIDGES AND THE CITY

Mayasum—The bridges—Sher Garhi palace—Mosque of Shah Hamadan—The great mosque—Hari Parbat—Tinpot temples.

To the east of Srinagar the hill called Takht-i-Sulaiman, or "Solomon's Throne," raises its trap summit a thousand feet above the Jehlam at its base. On the top of the ridge is the Sankar Acharya, a Hindu temple of great, but uncertain, age.

The river here flows to the west, and from its right or north bank runs, first to the north and then to the west, the Tsont-i-kul, a canal which re-enters the Jehlam lower down opposite Sher Garhi, and so forms an island called Mayasum. On this island, which is the European quarter, is the Residency, the dak bungalow, the post office, the telegraph office, the hotel, Dhanjibhoy's agent, the banks, and the shops for European goods. The island is protected from ordinary floods by a lofty embankment or bund, but it was all under water in September 1905, and in previous exceptional floods. They show you, in the dining-room of the hotel, where the water nearly reached the ceiling during these times. On the river bank opposite the island is the museum, a substantial square building of pyramidal elevation.

In this reach of the river the house-boats, upon which most of the resident sahibs live during the summer, are moored. From the 13th of December 1904, when the snow began to fall, up to the 1st of March 1905, there had been continual bad weather in the Kashmir valley, and the snowfall had been so heavy that many of the house-boats had been sunk at their moorings by the weight of the snow piled up on them. Many sahibs, instead of spending the summer on a house-boat, prefer to escape the mosquitoes and go to Gulmarg, "The Meadow of Roses," a hill station to the west of Srinagar on the northern slopes of the Pir Panjal 8500 feet above the sea.

There are three bridges across the Jehlam above

Photographed by the Author.

ZAINA KADAL, "THE FOURTH BRIDGE," SRINAGAR.

Srinagar. The first coming down the river is at Kanbal, not far from Islamabad which lies two miles back from the river, the second on Bij-Behara, and the third at Pampur. But the bridge below the museum in Srinagar, where the river turns to the north, is called "the first bridge" or Amiran Kadal, and close to this bridge on the left bank is the solidly-constructed Maharaja's Sher Garhi palace, and next to it the palace of General Raja Sir Amar Singh, brother of the Maharaja. The General's palace has an electric light installation, and the exterior is illuminated by arc-lights. A canal called the Kut-i-kul is cut from the left bank of the river below Sher Garhi to the Naya Kadal, and the canal is crossed a few yards from the river by the Tainki Kadal.

The next bridge over the Jehlam below Sher Garhi is called Haba Kadal, and then comes Fatteh Kadal towards the end of the reach to the north. Below the latter bridge on the right bank is the mosque of Shah Hamadan, built on the foundations of a Hindu temple in the reign of Kutab-ud-din in honour of the Saint Mir Sayyad Ali of Hamadan. The mosque is a square wooden building, with a balcony facing the river, covered by a shingle roof rising pyramid fashion to a square open pavilion with five arches on each side, and above this a pyramidal spire surmounted by an umbrella-shaped metal finial or ti. In the base of the spire above the pavilion are curious dormer windows with projecting tops, one in each face. The interior of the mosque is hung with embroidered cloths, and from the rafters are suspended ostrich eggs and crystal lustres. Shoes must be taken off to enter. Connected with the mosque are quaint wooden buildings, intended, we were told, for the priests.

From the Zaina Kadal we walked through filthy streets to the Jama Masjid, crossing a branch of the Mar Nullah, the canal which connects the Anchar Dal with the Astavol Dal and Boad Dal. The Jama Masjid is said to have been built by Sadr-ud-din in the year 1323. It was burnt twice and re-built the second time by Shah Jahan, burnt for the third time in 1671, and thoroughly repaired in 1816, only to be closed during the Sikh occupation between 1819 and 1845. The buildings, which are entirely of wood and are locally known as the

Photographed by the Author.

THE GREAT MOSQUE, SRINAGAR.

Ziarat (ziarat being the name for any Mohammedan shrine), are in a very bad state of repair and rapidly falling to pieces. They are no longer used for public worship, and we had difficulty in finding the caretaker; but after some delay the southern door, kept fastened with a padlock of the peculiar Kashmiri pattern, unlocked by a key which engages an interior screw, was opened for us. Within is a square enclosure like a sarai, surrounded by cloisters with a square building in the middle of each side. Three of these buildings have roofs and spires similar to the mosque of Shah Hamadan; and all of them have fine deodar pillars and rafters, the former at least 30 feet high, and said to be five hundred years old—in spite of the fires! In the centre of the enclosure is another wooden building.

A short distance to the north of the Jama Masjid is Hari Parbat, a hill about 250 feet high and 3 miles in circumference, surrounded by a wall 28 feet high, and having a fort on its summit. The wall was built by Akbar about the year 1590, and the enclosed hill was called the Nagar Nagar or Sangin Darwaza. The fort or citadel on the top is more modern, having been built by Atta Mohammed Khan, the Pathan governor.

There are several temples in Srinagar with domes and sikras covered over with pieces of biscuit tins. The most imposing of them all is the Srisanatan Dharm Sabha, in an enclosure on the left bank of the river, whose tinned sikras have small gilded spires. A short distance away on the same bank is the stone mosque built by Nur Jahan. On the right bank below the Zaina Kadal is the tomb of Zainu-l-abidin, the great king of Kashmir who came to the throne in the year 1417, and who died at the age of sixty-nine after a reign of fifty-two years. The bridge is named after the king, who built here the first permanent bridge, the bridges before his time being of boats.

At the Zaina Kadal the river takes a turn to the west, and below it are the Ali Kadal, the Naya Kadal, and last of all the Safa Kadal. The latter is a simple wooden arch ; but the others have piers, built of timbers, in the form of an inverted pyramid, each tier projecting beyond the one below, until the space between the piers is narrowed sufficiently to be spanned with long timbers. These bridges

Photographed by the Author.

HARI PARBAT, SRINAGAR.

ordinarily last from thirty to forty years, but in the flood of July 1893 six of the seven bridges were swept away, and only the Amiran Kadal was left standing. Except for these accidents, the number of bridges has remained unchanged for nearly five hundred years.

CHAPTER XIX

THE MOST BEAUTIFUL COUNTRY IN THE WORLD

Different points of view—From the steps of Solomon's Throne—The valley and the mountain barriers—Kashmir and the Kashmiris.

Kashmir is considered to be "one of the most beautiful and fertile valleys in the world," the "land of enchantment, the only land which never disappoints expectations"; "the most beautiful country in the East" and "the most lovely country under the sun." Of course we saw very little of it in our short stay; but what we did see was enough to make us desire to come again, and we saw nothing to cause us to disparage the reputation of the Happy Valley. The mountains enclosing the valley rival those of Switzerland, the lakes compare favourably with those of Westmoreland, and the poplar avenues recall the valley of the Loire. There are reminiscences of the Thames in the river,

Photographed by the Author.

TEMPLE DOME MADE FROM BISCUIT TINS, SRINAGAR.

suggestions of Venice in the town, and something of the quaint scenery of Holland in the flat country.

Opinions vary as to the best time to see Kashmir. Some say the summer, in spite of the heat and mosquitoes; some say the spring; but more favour the time when the ground is covered with snow. Resident sahibs, who had seen the valley at all seasons, gave us their opinions in the following words:—

"Unless you've come to select your nullah and get ready for a shooting expedition, you are much too early to see Kashmir to advantage. A fortnight hence the blossoms will be out and the whole scenery beautified. Or, better still, you should be here when the hills are covered with roses, when the fields are ablaze with the orange-coloured colchicum and the deep yellow saffron flowers, and when the gardens on the lake are gay with picnic parties and mem-sahibs in summer flocks flit through the groves." So said one sahib, and he recalled to mind Moore's lines:—

> "If woman can make the worst wilderness dear,
> Think, think what a heaven she must make of Cashmere."

But we heard a different story from an older sahib, who explained that the surveying parties we had seen on the right bank of the Jehlam, from the road up to Baramula, were engaged in the final surveys for the railway which would come up from Domel on that side, and which may be worked by electricity supplied by an installation utilising the water-power of the river. It was not yet known whether the connection with the North Western Railway would be made at Rawal Pindi or at Hasan Abdal, and through trains are not expected to run into the valley for at least five years. "Then," said he, "Kashmir will be utterly ruined. It has been spoilt by petticoats already. Before the tonga road was built, and the mem-sahibs began to come, we sahibs indeed lived a happy life. We had the finest sport, and the best the country afforded in the way of shelter, clothing, food, and women, and we found all of them good enough without importing any of these necessities. Then the mem-sahibs came, and now we must live in big houses, dress in fine linen, eat tinned food, and give up our bachelor ways! Why couldn't they leave well enough alone?"

Another sahib thought we were seeing the valley at its best when every hill was covered with snow and the flat floor of the valley, supposed to have been the bed of a lake in prehistoric times, was concealed under its white layers. "You can imagine the smaller beauties of blossoms and flowers, of green trees and yellow fields," he contended; "but you can't imagine the grander beauties of snow-clad mountains under a brilliant sun. The latter must be seen to understand and appreciate them." So we selected a brilliant afternoon to climb up the flank of "Solomon's Throne," far enough to get a good view of the valley and the ring of mountains surrounding it.

South from Sher Garhi on the left bank of the Jehlam a road runs to Shapiyon, where it turns to the south-west and crosses the Pir Panjal Pass, 11,400 feet above the sea, and the Ratan Pir. This is the old Imperial Road constructed in the early Mogul times on the left bank of the Pir Panjal stream, the more ancient road used by Akbar following the right bank, and it was between the two passes that Jahangir died in camp on Sunday October 28, 1627, on his way back from

Kashmir. The road continues by way of Nowshera on the Tawi River and through Bhimber to Gujrat, a station on the railway a few miles north of the Chenab River. Naba Pir, 14,066 feet, and Tatakuti, 15,524 feet, are seen to the west of Shapiyon; and other peaks of the Pir Panjal range are seen south-west of Srinagar, while to the west lies Gulmarg on the northern flank of the same range. North-west lies Baramula, and farther away the peak of Kazi Nag rises to the height of 12,125 feet. Coming around to the north is the range over which sportsmen after markhor travel through the Tragbal Pass, 11,770 feet above the sea, to the valley of the Kishanganga, and then by the Sarisangar Pass (13,900 feet) to the Astor Valley at the base of Nanga Parbat, or Dayarmar, which rises 26,629 feet above the sea, and can be seen due north of Gulmarg. Astor is about 150 miles from Srinagar and is reached in fourteen marches, Gilgit is 230 miles or twenty-two marches.

North of Srinagar are the Drawar mountains among whose peaks is Haramukh, which rises to the height of 16,903 feet. Nearly twenty-five miles away to the north-north-west is Safapur

Photographed by the Author.

ON THE RIVER, SRINAGAR.

(10,296 feet). Nearer at hand towards the east follow Sayaha (11,318 feet), Mahadeo (13,073 feet), and Batgul (14,409 feet). The Sind valley lies on the other side of the last three peaks, and up this valley is the road, 237 miles long—by the Zoji La 11,300 feet above the sea in the Bara Lacha range and the passes of Namika La (13,000 feet), and Futu La (13,400 feet)—to Leh, which lies at an elevation of 11,500 feet in Ladakh five miles from the Indus. This is the road which starts north from Srinagar and is taken by those who desire to add the Ovis Ammon to their trophies. Gwash Brari (17,830 feet) lies behind the ridge to the east of Srinagar, and south of this ridge are the peaks of Ganderpater (14,500 feet) and Churu (11,332 feet), behind a nearer range which terminates to the south in the Wastarwan mountain (9707 feet), at whose foot, fifteen miles to the south-east, runs the road up the right bank of the Jehlam to Islamabad and on by the Banihal Pass (9200 feet) to Jammu, 177 miles by road from Srinagar. By the Sidau route the distance between the capitals is under 130 miles. Even in midsummer the highest peaks would show a crest of snow, but when we saw them they were covered down to their bases, and in the whole valley the only places not covered with snow were the waterways and the mountain precipices, too steep to give the snow a resting place.

The distant views were certainly grand and impressive, and the glimpses nearer at hand brilliant and beautiful, so that we were entirely satisfied with our hasty survey of the valley.

The people did not impress us so favourably. From the time of Hiuen Tsiang, the Chinese traveller, who resided in the valley of "Kia-shi-mi-lo" for two years in the early half of the seventh century and described the people as "handsome in appearance," the beauty of the women of Kashmir has been the theme of Eastern poets and prose writers; and six centuries ago Marco Polo, the first European to write of them, said "the women of Kashmir are very beautiful." From his time to that of Fredric Drew, who thirty years ago found "the general run of women decidedly good-looking," there is no discordant note in the chorus of admiration. Perhaps all the good-looking women now keep parda, or perhaps the people have degenerated, but for some reason or other we saw nothing of feminine beauty. Some of the children we saw were nice-looking, but that was all.

The Kashmiris are of a race similar to the Pathans, and their features are strikingly Jewish. The girls are married as early as the age of seven, and cohabitation is general at twelve and sometimes as early as nine. They are usually mothers by the time they are fourteen, and as they are very prolific, bearing from ten to fourteen children, they age quickly. Moreover, great numbers of them are pitted with small-pox, and as it is not thought quite respectable for a woman to be clean they are almost invariably filthy-looking, so that there is not much that is attractive about the Kashmiri beauties.

The Kashmiri women of to-day use, as they did centuries ago, a black powder of lead ore called kohol to darken their eyelids, and even babies may be seen in Srinagar, as in some of the cities of the plains, with eyes heavily blackened with it. Men and women wear the pheran, a tunic or gown with hanging sleeves fastened at the neck and falling to the ankles. Under this gown is carried in winter a kangar, or fire-basket. This is really a portable stove, being a fireproof—usually clay—basin, containing burning charcoal, enclosed in a basket with a handle. Held under the gown in the neighbourhood of the stomach, the kangar does not improve the appearance of the natives. The coolies wear palahru, which are straw sandals almost exactly like the Japanese waraji, and these sandals are the very best footgear for mountain work, particularly in wet weather.

The Kashmiris have a very ancient and continuous literary history contained in four chronicles called the Rajatarangini, after the title of the first of them which was begun by the poet Kalhana in 1148 A.D. The others date from 1459, 1486, and 1586, respectively. When Akbar conquered the valley in 1586-8, a copy of these chronicles in Sanskrit was handed to him, and he had them translated, and they have been done into French by Troyer, and into English by Jogesh Chunder Dutt, M. A. Stein, and others.

The Kashmiris remained subject to the Moguls from Akbar's time until the Afghans under Ahmed Shah Durani captured Kashmir in 1752; and the

Photographed by the Author.

RIVERSIDE SCENE, SRINAGAR.

Afghans or Pathans ruled in the valley until 1819, when the Sikhs under Ranjit Singh conquered it. Gulab Singh, a Dogra Rajput, was given the rajaship of Jammu, but the Kashmir valley itself was ruled by Sikh governors. In 1846, after the British had defeated the Sikhs, Kashmir was sold to the Maharaja of Jammu for £750,000. Gulab Singh died in 1857 and was succeeded by his third son Ranbir Singh. Ranbir died in September 1885, and his eldest son, Partab Singh, the present Maharaja, began his reign. Partab Singh failed to rule in a manner satisfactory to the Indian Government, and he was obliged in 1889 to resign all his powers to a Council; but in 1891 the Maharaja was given a greater share in the direction of affairs, and in 1905 his full powers were restored.

And so it is that for over three centuries the Kashmiris have been subject to an alien rule and slaves to the tender mercies of a succession of governors, nominally representing the conquerors for the time being, but in reality free from all responsibility and at liberty to practice any injustice or cruelty upon the defenceless people.

That the Kashmiris should have developed in a marked degree the traits common to all ill-used slaves is not surprising; but their best friends hope that the new era inaugurated by the land settlement of 1887-93 may witness a gradual amelioration in their social condition and a corresponding improvement in their character.

Besides "man's inhumanity to man" the Kashmiris have suffered from small-pox and cholera epidemics; from famines, such as the one in 1877-9 when there was no road for wheeled conveyances into the Kashmir valley; and from earthquakes, of which the most severe recorded was in 1885, when there was a series of shocks lasting from the 13th of May to the 16th of August, during which period over 3500 people perished. And now the plague is reported to be again raging in Jammu.

CHAPTER XX

THE GARDENS OF THE GREAT MOGULS

Rotten Row—The City Lake—Nishat Bagh—Shalimar Bagh—Lalla Rookh—Nasim Bagh.

At eight o'clock in the morning of the day we visited the pleasure-gardens of the Moguls on the lakes to the north-east of Srinagar, the thermometer outside of our window stood at 28° F., and it had been two degrees lower during the night. We took shikaras at the bridge close to the east end of the poplar avenue, known as Rotten Row, and paddled through the Tsont-i-kul, or "Apple-tree Canal," to the Boad Dal.

Rotten Row is comparatively new, and takes the place of the old poplar avenue, planted by the Sikhs, which was a mile and a furlong in length and fifty-six feet wide. The Boad Dal, or City Lake, is under four miles long and only a little over two and a half miles wide. The bottom is covered with a dense growth of aquatic plants, and the famous "floating gardens" have been made by cutting these plants off below the surface, sprinkling earth over the matted top and planting vegetables. At the time we saw them, these floating gardens simply looked like the flat surface of a marsh slightly elevated above the level of the lake. Around the lake are orchards, vineyards, and hop-fields, and at the northern end of the eastern shore is the Nishat Bagh. This garden, 1800 feet long and containing about forty-four acres, is laid out in terraces, rising back from the lake nearly to the high road on the flank of the hills above, through the centre of which a stream of water is led in cascades and fountains to the pavilion near the entrance. In the pavilion are carved window screens, some glass windows, and a lacquered papier-maché ceiling, and there are fountains in the square, open courtyard. The garden is planted with cherry-trees and chenars; and roses, lilacs, and syringas grow there in profusion. Across the lake in front of the Nishat Bagh is a curious little humpbacked bridge over

Photographed by the Author.

OUR PARTY LEAVING SRINAGAR BY HOUSE-BOAT.

which runs the road from Srinagar to the Hindu temple at Ishibori, half a mile to the north of the Nishat Bagh. At Ishibori the Hindus have a great bathing festival, where "mixed bathing" *in puris naturalibus*, or *netnun* as the Kashmiris would say, may be seen.

From Nishat Bagh we passed through an archway in the Sutoo, as the causeway between the two lakes is called, and paddled up the Astavol Dal to the canal leading to the Shalimar Bagh. The upper part of the canal was dry, so we left the boat and walked. The banks of the canal are planted with chenars, or plane-trees, mulberry-trees, and "tooth-cleaning-trees," as our manjhi called the elm-trees from whose wood the "tooth-sticks" are made, and beyond the trees are paddy-fields.

Perhaps there is no garden in the world so famous as the Shalimar Bagh, built on the bank of the Astavol Dal by Jahangir and further embellished by Shah Jahan. It was the favourite retreat of the former Emperor and his Empress, Nur Jahan—the Nur Mahal or "Light of the Harem," of Thomas Moore's *Lalla Rookh.*

Lalla Rookh herself was a daughter of Aurangzeb, grandson of Jahangir. Shalimar is not a botanical garden, but a park of fine chenar, walnut, willow, poplar, and elm-trees through which is diverted a stream upon whose artificial banks are built a number of summer-houses or pavilions.

In the lake face of the rectangular enclosure are two gateways which lead through lodges placed on either side of the central line of the garden, which is a third of a mile in length. Inside the gates and facing them are two pavilions joined by an arcade of twelve pillars, and behind the arcade a group of fifteen fountains. Then a pair of small pavilions, one on each side of the central canal, another pair of similar pavilions, and then the main pavilion or principal baradari with a triple roof. This is surrounded by basins from which rise fountains, twenty-one in front, sixty-three on each side, and twenty-seven in back, or one hundred and seventy-four fountains in all. The sides of the basins in back and in front of the baradari have niches for holding lights. The plinth of the baradari is of polished black limestone resembling black marble. Within there are three chambers in a line from side to side, the central oblong chamber has a ceiling painted in panels, and the side chambers have coloured glass windows. There are porticoes or verandas in front and back, supported by black marble pillars with carved bases and bracket capitals, four simple ones in the centre and double pillars at the corners. The ceilings of the verandas are painted in panels, and the upper half of the wall is also painted. Among the decorations are barasingh heads holding a lamp on each tine.

Behind the baradari is a small pavilion which is said to have been the zenana, and there is a larger one on either side; while there are buildings at the sides of the garden in a line with each of the pair of detached pavilions, so that, not counting the gate lodges, there are thirteen buildings in the grounds. It was snowing when we left Shalimar Bagh, and we paddled across the lake in a snowstorm to the Nasim Bagh or "Garden of Zephyrs," begun in Akbar's time and now famous for its grove of chenars. The chenar, or boin, specimens of which measure over sixty feet around the trunk, is the plane-tree, which is said to have been introduced into Kashmir by Ali Mardan Khan, who was subahdar or governor under Shah Jahan, and who laid out the terraces of the other Shalimar Bagh in the suburbs of Lahore. His tomb may be seen on the way from Lahore to the gardens. From the Garden of Zephyrs we went to see the painted wooden mosque at Hazrat Bal, the most sacred Mohammedan shrine in Kashmir, where they were repeating the afternoon prayers, and back by the Miphal and Tsont-i-kul through the sluice-gate to the landing-place behind the golf-course and hotel. It cleared up later, and we took a walk out by the road which runs to the south of Takht-i-Sulaiman, then turns to the north-east across the shoulder of the hill and runs north to Nishat and Shalimar. We left this road, struck across the fields to the Anatnag road, which runs south-east up the Jehlam valley to Islamabad—which the natives call Anatnag or Anantbag—and returned by the Ram Munshi Bagh and the Bund.

Photographed by the Author.

KASHMIRI BEAUTIES.

CHAPTER XXI

SRINAGAR TO BARAMULA

Manjhis and nautch-girls—The "river of milk"—The Naru canal—Winter birds—Singharas—Volur Lake.

When we left Srinagar we engaged a house-boat to take us as far as Baramula, and took on board stores for a three days' picnic. The boatman arranged the whole "bandobast," and provided an English house-boat for ourselves and a dunga, or native house-boat, to be used as kitchen and to accommodate the crew. The charge for the boats was one rupee eight annas per day, the use of cooking utensils eight annas, and the hire of eight coolies at four annas each came to two rupees, making a total charge of four rupees per day. This seemed very reasonable, although a dunga can be hired for twenty to thirty rupees a month, but we found that the "eight coolies" meant the boatman's family, and included his wife, a young man with a frock-coat who was above any work, and an old man who was incapable of any. The boatman is usually called by the Hindustani name manjhi, but the Kashur name is hanji or hanz. The Srinagar manjhi combines in himself the professions of water-man, interpreter, guide, and procurer, so we were not surprised when we boarded the house-boat to find three nautch-girls engaged for our entertainment on the way down. We declined their services, however, and dismissed them with an honorarium, after taking their photographs seated in the doorway of the house-boat.

It took over six hours to do the ten miles from the Tsont-i-kul to Shadipur. After passing the Safa Kadal the Dudganga or "river of milk" joins the Jehlam on the left (*khowar*) bank; and opposite Shadipur, where there is a suspension bridge with brick towers, the Sind river, which flows down from the Zoji La, enters the Jehlam from the east or right (*dachan*) bank. Shadipur was founded in the latter half of the fourteenth century by Sultan Shahabu-d-din, after whom it was called Shahabuddinpur. The six miles from Shadipur to Sumbal Bridge was done in about two hours, and we seemed to get quite close to Aha Tyung, an isolated hill rising 1000 feet above the plain, at whose northern base is the famous Manusbal Lake. By going through the Naru Canal below Shadipur we cut off about sixteen miles and reduced our voyage to two days or about twenty hours drifting.

The first day we walked many miles along the bank, and from time to time as we came in sight of native women drawing water from the river, we noticed that they dropped their lotas and chattis which they had filled with water and fled precipitately towards their villages. These strange proceedings in a country where the sahib is a frequent visitor, led us to think that perhaps the foreign nimrods had not exclusively hunted the beasts and the birds. Of the latter we saw a great variety and large numbers. There were golden eagles, vultures, falcons, hawks, and kites (*chil*): cranes, egrets, and blue-crested herons, the latter preserved for the use of the Maharaja. The Kashmiri call it the breg, and the plume of heron feathers worn as a mark of distinction is called gund. The Indian kingfisher flashed his turquoise-blue and orange-brown plumage before the bow of our boat, and the pied kingfisher flew along the banks of the stream. Finches with black and yellow feathers, hoopoes, and a solitary golden oriole or "mango-bird" darted through the air; and floating over the water were flocks of the white-headed krind or laughing gulls.

At noon the second day we saw a large jhil to the south-west alive with wild ducks. The natives called them *keus*, *nilig*, and *honk*, which would be teal, mallard, and shoveller ducks, and they shoot them with long match-lock muskets firmly lashed to boats and aimed by steering the latter. Two and a half hours later, when we were in the south-west corner of Volur Lake, we saw to the north large flocks of grey geese, which the boatmen called *ans*. Volur Lake is the largest in India, and is in reality an expansion of the Jehlam, which enters it at the south-east end and flows out from the south-west. In times of low water the lake measures about 13 miles by 6 and covers an area of 78 square miles, but at times of flood it covers over 100 square miles.

On the lake we found a number of boats con-

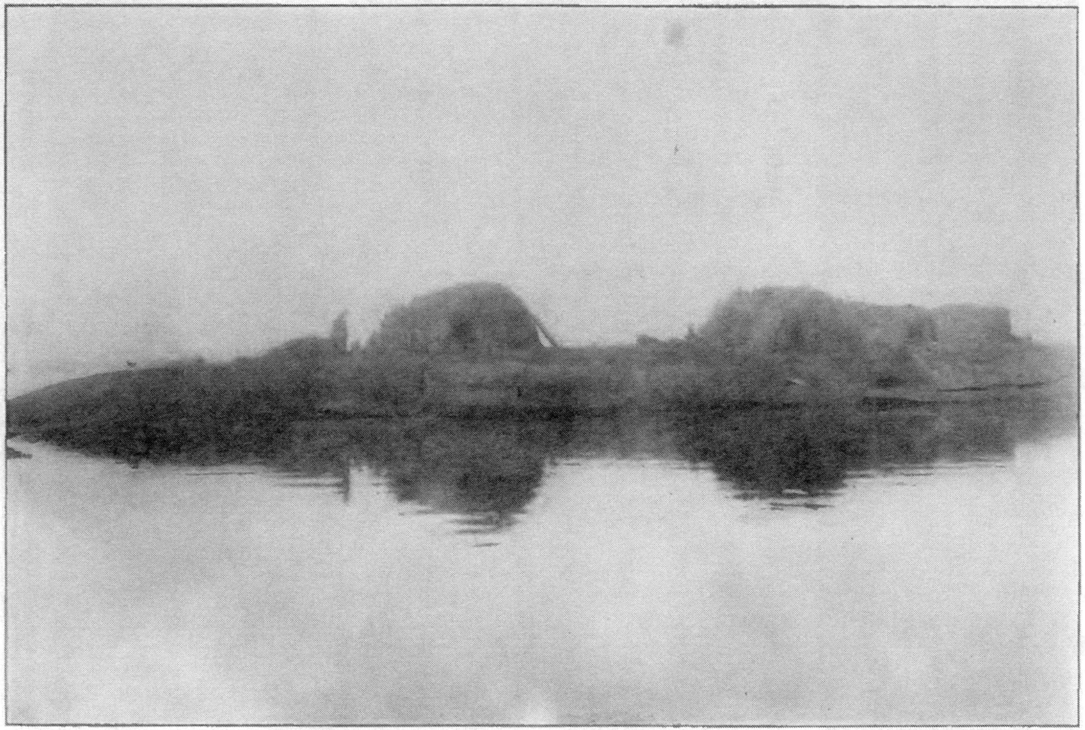

Photographed by the Author.

A VILLAGE ON THE NARU CANAL, KASHMIR.

taining fishermen who were using a sort of hoe on a long pole (*kamkhuru*) to gather great quantities of singharas (caltrops) which grow on the bottom of the lake. These are heart-shaped water-nuts with four curved horns measuring 3 to 4 inches between their extremities. The nuts are dried, pounded, ground into flour, and made into a sort of bread which is eaten by the poorer people. The shells are utilised as a fuel which is called kanga.

From other fishermen we bought mahsir, which they called *pairim gad* ("Punjab fish"). The mahsir is a carp with a greenish-brown back and bronze sides, which is, however, more like a salmon in shape. It is the great sporting fish of India, and has been known to attain the weight of 150 pounds; but 40 pounds is a good ordinary size, and those we saw in the Kashmir only ran to about 4 pounds. Cooked when freshly caught the mahsir is an excellent fish for the table.

Our manjhi prepared for us very palatable meals, and we found that the Kashmiri names for breakfast, lunch, and dinner are *nipari*, *mimuz*, and *battakheu*. We had bought such tinned things as we thought we should require, and sufficient whisky to last to Rawal Pindi. We knew that the lexicographers traced the word whisky to the Gaelic word uisge, meaning water; and we had heard that Scotch whisky was prepared in a pot still from malted barley. We had never seen the process, and were unable to say whether the whisky with a Scotch name we bought at Srinagar was derived from water or barley; but it is curious that the Kashmiri name for barley is wiska.

Our manjhi's little bill for the supplies he considered it necessary to lay in for a trip of forty-eight hours was, in English weights and prices, as follows :—

Item	£	s.	d.
720 pounds of wood	£0	4	0
16 „ meat	0	4	0
10 „ potatoes	0	0	10
2 „ onions	0	0	6
2 „ butter	0	1	4
4 „ rice and dhal	0	1	4
3 „ flour	0	0	8
5 „ milk	0	0	8
4 „ mahsir	0	1	0
12 loaves of bread	0	2	0
4 dozen eggs	0	1	0
5 ducks	0	1	8
4 water jars	0	0	8
Green vegetables	0	1	0
Salt, pepper, curry powder, etc.	0	2	0
	£1	2	8

Photographed by the Author.

DUCK-HUNTER NEAR SOPUR, KASHMIR.

(He is re-winding his turban to be photographed. His musket, lashed to the boat, projects forward.)

The quantities were in most cases more than twice as much as we consumed, and the prices, which certainly looked cheap enough, were, according to the lists posted in the dak bungalow, two to three times what should have been paid. For example, the current price for ducks is twopence each, for eggs, twopence a dozen, and for twopence you can buy about a pound and a half of meat, two pounds of rice, four pounds of potatoes, or forty pounds of firewood.

After traversing the south-western corner of Volur Lake we got into the Jehlam again, and three-quarters of an hour later arrived at Sopur Bridge. Four miles below Sopur the Pohur enters the Jehlam, and from Sopur there is a road to Gulmarg, which is eighteen miles from Sopur and seventeen miles from Baramula. We stopped long enough at Sopur to visit the old mosque on the left bank of the river, and the bazaars on the right bank, and left at half-past five, tying up for the night two hours later. It took three hours to get to Baramula Bridge the next morning. The natives we saw coming down from Srinagar seemed more sullen and more apathetic than the city folk. The huts of the villagers were miserable to a degree, and the villagers themselves equally miserable and filthy.

CHAPTER XXII

AND SO HOME

Baramula to Rawal Pindi—The last dak

AT Baramula we left the boat and transferred our belongings, mostly packed in yakdans or mule-trunks, which we bought for about ten shillings each at Srinagar, to the pack-animals which had been provided for us by the tahsildar, to whom we had previously telegraphed. The pack-ponies are called *markhban* and the pack-donkeys *kharwala.* The *khar* or *kharwar*, a donkey's load, is the ancient standard weight of Kashmir, and is nearly one hundred and eighty pounds. We arranged with Dhanjibhoy's agent to have a special tonga to meet us at Uruboha, and about eleven o'clock our cavalcade left Baramula, the boat people coming to see us off and say *hawalat khuda* (adieu).

Six months later, in September 1905, almost

the whole town of Baramula was destroyed by a fire which raged for twelve hours. Eight hundred houses are said to have been burnt, and the damage was estimated at over £50,000.

As our pace was limited by that of our pack-animals, it took us over five hours to ride from Baramula down to Rampur, so that we only averaged three miles an hour. A large number of coolies were at work on the road, and it had been greatly improved in the few days since we passed over it coming up. For long distances a pathway had been cut in the snow and ice; much of the fallen rock had been removed; and the larger boulders, too big to be hauled off the road, were being drilled preparatory to blasting. Men were stationed at some of the more dangerous places to warn travellers that the landslides were still moving.

On the Kashmir road, as well as in many parts of India, the custom prevails of two men working a spade or shovel. One of them pushes the spade in, and the other helps the removal of the earth or rock by hauling on a rope attached to the lower end of the handle.

Photographed by the Author.

LOOKING NORTH-EAST OVER VOLUR LAKE, KASHMIR.

After some food at Rampur we pushed on; but at one place where there had been a big avalanche of snow, between milestones 82 and 81, our pack-mules had to be unloaded and led across. This proved to be the last obstruction to the working of the tongas, and at Uruboha we transferred overselves and luggage to the tonga waiting for us, and leaving at six o'clock did the eleven miles to Uri in an hour and a half. How we rejoiced to hear again the steady clank of the yoke on the tonga pole, and the sibilant call of the driver, like whistling the letter S, as he urged his horses over the broken road—the latter half of the journey in the deepening twilight. The day had been fine; but we had hardly settled down to our dinner before it began to rain, and the downpour continued all night and until we left Garhi after tiffin the next day.

The purple and yellow five-petalled wild-flowers were in bloom from Uri down, and trees were in blossom farther along the road. Near Uppi there had been a heavy rock-fall since we had passed up, and there were fresh falls in other places. When we reached Domel the sun had come out, and we met a procession of men armed with swords marching behind a drummer. All the way down the hillsides are cultivated wherever the slopes are not too steep, and every karewa has its paddy-fields. Goats and jungle-crows were both plentiful, but there was otherwise little animal life seen after leaving Baramula. We drove steadily on to Kohala, and found we had accomplished nearly seventy miles in about ten hours, or, deducting the hour for tiffin, in nine hours including all other stops.

The next morning we started early from Kohala for the long grind up to Bagla, which, including stops, we only did at the rate of five miles an hour As we got near Bagla the snow reappeared first on the hillside next to the road, and then in places on the road itself, and finally all over the road and the trees near it. At Bagla we found a lot of good coolies, and, employing two extra ones to take turn about, we made excellent time up, arriving at Trinity Church in two hours and eighteen minutes. For this walk, however, we had provided ourselves with alpenstocks and with nail-studded leather sandals or chaplies (*tsapli*) strapped over our boots, so that we got on very comfortably.

Nothing had been done to improve the road over Murree since we came up from Rawal Pindi, and a great block of stone effectually blocked the tonga road, half a mile beyond Bagla. Just after milestone 43 we left the tonga road, zigzagged up the mountain for half an hour, and got into the level road around the north flank. After milestone 39 at the cross-roads we continued uphill, passing the monument to Captain G. A. de Visme, 8th Hussars, who was killed here on June 20, 1880. At Murree we wasted a lot of time over tiffin, but got down to the Brewery in thirty-five minutes, found a tonga waiting for us, and left the Brewery for Rawal Pindi about half-past four. A couple of ox-carts in the road above Gohragully delayed us while their loads were removed and the carts hauled to one side in the snow, but below Gohragully the road was free from snow and we did the next fifteen miles down in an hour and three-quarters. We left the last dak at 7.40 P.M., the lights of Rawal Pindi were already in sight, and we were figuring on the exact minute we would arrive at the hotel and what we should have for dinner, when our off-pony took it into his head to turn nasty. For nearly two hours he kept wheeling around from one ditch to the other, despite the united efforts of the driver, the syce, and the three passengers, and in the end had to be unharnessed and sent back while we waited in the dark for another relay, and it was after ten o'clock when we finally arrived at the hotel.

Over the evening meal we congratulated ourselves upon having succeeded in obtaining a peep at the romantic country in the bosom of the Himalayas, and the pleasantest recollections will always be associated with our excursion from Rawal Pindi to Srinagar and the Happy Valley of Kashmir.

INDEX

Geographical names in small capitals. Names of gods, persons, monuments, scenes and subjects in Roman characters. Other foreign words in italics. Anc. = ancient. B. = Burma or Burmese. K. = Kashmir, Kashmiri, or Kashur.